JOHNNY APPLESEED

[See page 101

RESTING HIS ELBOWS ON THE HEARTH, HE READ FROM THE BIBLE

JOHNNY APPLESEED

THE ROMANCE OF THE SOWER

BY

ELEANOR ATKINSON

AUTHOR OF

Greyfriars Bobby

WITH ILLUSTRATIONS BY
FRANK T. MERRILL

Fredonia Books
Amsterdam, The Netherlands

Johnny Appleseed:
The Romance of the Sower

by
Eleonor Atkinson

ISBN: 1-4101-0896-1

Reprinted from the 1915 edition

Fredonia Books
Amsterdam, The Netherlands
http://www.fredoniabooks.com

TO
THE AMERICAN PIONEERS

CONTENTS

CONTENTS

ILLUSTRATIONS

FOREWORD

APPLE-BLOSSOMS that gladdened the hearts, and fruits that brought comfort and pleasure to the rude firesides of the earliest settlers in the Middle West, were the living memorials of an apostle of beauty, peace and social service who is now almost forgotten.

Explorer, missionary, fur-trader and conqueror preceded Jonathan Chapman, the nurseryman of Puritan breed, whose identity was lost in the devoted " Johnny Appleseed." His day was that of the pioneers who crossed the Alleghany Mountains; of the river boatmen who navigated the uncharted waterways of the old Northwest Territory, and of the Indian-fighters of the last border wars. All of these played their honorable parts in the winning of an empire of forest and prairie. But no one of them labored with greater courage, over such a large region of country, or toiled with the unselfishness and untiring zeal of this heroic orchardist. Half mystic, half poet, a lover of nature and of his fellow-men, his long life of solitary and perilous wandering, always in the van

1

FOREWORD

of migration, was consecrated to the blossoming of the wilderness.

Three-quarters of a century ago he was still a loved and revered guest in the cabins of our grandfathers. His orchards lived after him. Some of his trees may be standing to-day; but the man who planted them has receded to a dim, legendary figure. Let us recover what may be known of him, restore him to his time and place, recall the almost incredible conditions under which he did his inspired task. Let us give him again his meed of love and gratitude for a beautiful life of self-sacrifice that asked no reward, and that came, in old age, to some end obscure and lonely.

JOHNNY APPLESEED

JOHNNY APPLESEED

I

THE FRONTIER ORCHARD

JOHNNY had known the night before that warm showers would bring out a rosy foam of apple-blossoms, so all through the soft spring darkness he had slept on the bench in the sapling stoop that shaded his cabin door, where he would awake to the incense from the orchard. That surf of bloom, tossing in the wind of dawn and scattering a scented spray of raindrops, was the first thing his eyes rested upon. But he was aroused, as was every one in the frontier town of Pittsburg on that April morning in the last year of the eighteenth century, by

the blowing of bugles from boat-yards, landings and ferries along the water-front.

The rivers had risen in the night. In the
days before weather-reports snow melted on
the mountains unnoted, and floods fell un-
prophesied down the valleys of the Allegheny
and Monongahela. If both streams rose at
once, at a time when the tide of westward
migration was at its height, the bugles blew
for the men of the town to be up and stirring.
There was a procession of emigrants to be fer-
ried across to Ohio, and river craft, that had
lain stranded in back-water since the going
down of the last freshet, to be swiftly loaded
and set adrift.

All this bustle of arrival and departure
would bring a rush of business to every warehouse, outfitting store and craft-shop along
the terraced and gullied banks. Therefore,
at the blare of the bugles, the log-and-plank-
built town of fifteen hundred people, that was
wedged in the muddy fork of the swollen
streams, swarmed like an untidy ant-hill.
And up on the wooded slopes to the east,
men who had been delayed by low water ran
out of camps and back again, seeing the
need of haste in getting their families, ani-

mals and goods down to the boat and ferry landings.

To Jonathan Chapman, orchardist, these matters were of small concern. He was, possibly, the only man living in Pittsburg who would not be counting his gains at the end of the day, although no other had such attractive wares to offer as he. But he could not honestly sell young apple-trees that would die on the long, slow journeys into the wilderness of the Northwest Territory, so he was obliged to discourage men from buying. Nevertheless he would have as busy a day as any, just in being a little brother to wayfaring man and beast.

His nursery and orchard lay on the main-traveled road, on the brow of Grant's Hill, the very first bit of rising ground eastward of the town. From that green and flowery slope the ancient woods had long since retreated, so from rude doorways below, from forest camps above, and from boats on the flanking, bluff-bordered streams Johnny's blossoming trees were visible that morning as a drift of dawn. To the nearer view of passers-by the nurseryman and his orchard offered a moment of rest and refreshment from the feverish activities

3

of the day. Every traveler stopped at his gate, for in a never-failing spring that bubbled up, cold and clear, in a cobble-lined basin by the roadside, Johnny had "next water" in and out of Pittsburg.

People who lived in the region cheerfully went a mile out of their way to water their animals at that famous spring and to have the pleasure of passing the time of day with Johnny. Incoming horses found that mossy fountain with their noses as soon as they broke through the forest wall.

The first team of the morning's procession came down the steep road on the run; and when the horses stopped of their own accord, with mouths plunged deep in the pool, two people looked out of the clumsy covered wagon in delighted surprise. To travelers who had seen nothing for two hundred miles except mountains, forests, brawling streams, and now and then a God-forgotten cabin, the squalid town below seemed incredibly big and friendly and reassuring. But that was a day of fierce independence and land-hunger, when it was the dream of men to hew out homes in the Western wilds. Pittsburg was but the Gateway to the West, a place to be gone

4

through and left behind. This young home-
seeker gave but one glance to the town and
then turned back to the dream-come-true of
Johnny's orchard. It was a heartening thing
to find it there, fronting the unbroken woods
and unbridled flood.

"If this don't look for all the world like a
farm in Little Old Rhody!"

The still younger, homesick wife, scared
white and thin by weeks of wild travel, cried,
"O-o-oh!" clutched her husband's arm, swallowed hard, and stared as at a vision. It was
a home of long security, of peace and beauty,
such as she had not hoped ever to see again.
Indeed, the orchards of grudging New England made no such growth or lavish promises
as this that bowered Johnny's little gray-and-
brown nest of a mill-slab cabin. And no-
where in the East was to be seen such a vast
apple-tree, like a forest oak, as flung its blos-
somy banners out over picket fence, pool
and roadway.

Before the horses had finished drinking
Johnny came whistling down the path. He
was extraordinarily happy because he had so
much to share. There were seasons when he
had nothing besides cold water and a friendly

word. But this morning he had a heap of wrinkled, winey apples, brought up from winter pits, at the gate, and his orchard was a thing of breathless beauty to delight the eyes of all comers.

A slenderly built and beardless young man of twenty-four, in the rough garb of the frontier, Johnny was in no way remarkable except for gentleness of speech and manners, and for sympathetic understanding of other people's difficulties. There was tribute to the courage of these pilgrims in the way he lifted his hat of felted rabbit fur, and offered help in his hand-clasp. He had bought this place, which dated from the days of old Fort Pitt, at the close of the Indian War five years before; and the stream of migration that had flowed by his gate to enter upon a long struggle in Ohio was, to him, an inspiring but poignant thing.

Now a youth who has his feet set in some safe and pleasant way of living must needs be looking for the dear other-self to share it. And where was Johnny to look, in that day when romance set sail from all Eastern ports and voyaged westward, if not in these canvas-spread ships of the mountains? But if he glanced first into the Conestoga wagon, with eyes unconsciously eager, he was, in the next instant, offering the best of the withered fruit and breaking a spray from the great tree.

"For me!" stammered the young woman. "You are robbing yourself of the harvest."

"It is a wild tree; my big bouquet. The French officers at old Fort Duquesne brought comforts from Canada, and they had gay picnics on this hillside. The tree must have grown from an apple-core that was thrown away. The fruit is as tough and bitter as a crab-apple of the woods, but the blossoms have a deeper color and richer fragrance than those of the tame trees."

They all looked up through the branches that were flung in rugged and pink profusion against the sky. And neither the half-century-old tree, nor the orchard that was planted when the victory at Yorktown was still good news, looked to be more securely or joyously rooted in that soil than did Johnny. The woman saw that, and something wistful in her face made the man grip her hand and speak with bluff tenderness:

"We'll have a place in Ohio like this, one of these days, little woman."

"Oh, let's have it now!" she cried. She was so young, and life so long. It stretched before her, down that broad vale, so wild and lonely.

Johnny was comforting the horses with apples, and trying not to see or hear a plea that tugged at his own heartstrings. It was unlikely that people of this first generation in the backwoods of Ohio would be able to have orchards around their stark and comfortless cabins in the clearings. So many were going out in that vain belief. So many would have the hope kindled in their breasts this morning by the sight of his blossoming trees. A little gray cloud obscured the sun for a moment, dimming the perfect blue and gold of the morning.

Now and then one of the lion-hearted men who opened the iron trails to the West had a glimpse of what the loved woman suffered; and when he had it his own resolution broke as a tree cracks in the frost. This was not the first emigrant who had turned to Johnny and asked, in a voice gone husky:

"Is this place for sale?"

Johnny shook his head. The question was asked almost daily. To a man on horseback he could say, "There isn't enough money in Uncle Sam's treasury to buy my orchard." But to the man in a wagon, with a family, he said, compassionately, "I wish I could give you one just like it." No one ever doubted his sincerity, or ever forgot the look of brotherly love from his dark-gray, black-lashed eyes when he said it. To the most eager and intelligent he offered a small buckskin bag of seeds, with the plea, "Won't you try to grow some apple-trees for yourself?"

This man wisely refused the gift. The growing of nursery stock was a business in itself, and he would have all he could do for the next few years to save their souls alive. By the time he could care properly for young fruit-trees he thought there would be nurserymen in Ohio.

Again Johnny shook his head. "Not for a generation, except perhaps in Marietta and Cincinnati. Really to serve the pioneers scattered and lost in that forty thousand square miles of forest, an orchardist would have to have the courage and zeal of John the Baptist."

There was a gasping sigh from the woman. She suddenly reached for the little bag of seeds and put it in the bosom of her homespun gown. They drove away slowly, but looking back, as so many did; and, as he so often did, Johnny ran after them. It would be a weary day on the crowded river-bank. Wouldn't the young wife rather rest under his trees?

She was over the wheel in a moment, and she never stopped running until she stood, shining-eyed, under that canopy of wondrous bloom. Rustic benches and stools were in the orchard for expected guests, but for this appealing visitor who had special need of ease, Johnny went into the house to fetch a Franklin chair. He had bought it in Philadelphia for the Puritan grandmother who had come out with him from Boston. Now that she lay under a grassy mound in the orchard, the chair had the air of waiting for another occupant.

A little, low, splint-bottomed rocker, it was so lightly balanced that a breeze through an opening door set it in motion. Johnny never saw it so without also seeing in it a young wife and mother. She was surely coming to him, as a bird to its nest, perhaps on this very wave of migration that was now breaking over the mountain wall. The fire was laid ready for

"HOW LONG MUST WE WAIT FOR OUR ORCHARD?"

her on the hearth, the house was swept, the
cellar stored, the spining-wheel oiled. For
her the apple-trees blossomed and fruited,
the bees gathered nectar, and a pure and
steady flame burned in Johnny's heart.

He stopped the chair gently as it rocked
in the breeze, and when he brought it out his
visitor's first musing speech sank into his
thoughts as water sinks into the grateful
earth:

"How happy a woman could be here with
a brood of little children." She laid her
hand in the low crotch of a sprawling tree.
"I had one like this to climb into when I
was a child. How long must we wait for our
orchard?"

"Not so many years as in New England—
if you have luck with your seeds. Don't
count upon that too much."

So many things had happened to trees that
he had sold and seeds that he had given away,
to disappoint hopes!

He told her something of the letters that had
come back to him from forest clearings. For
a moment of revulsion she leaned her head
against the dear tree, with closed eyes and
quivering lips. Then she looked up with the

bright bravery that in pioneer women was one of God's miracles.

"Nothing must happen to my seeds. I could not bear it, because—"

She held up a tiny, unfinished garment of tow linen for him to see. Men and women and children told the secrets of their hearts to Johnny. She began at once to sew, and to hum a lullaby, as she rocked in his little chair.

Another caravan was at the gate. For three hours Johnny was kept busy stuffing hands and pockets with apples, breaking sprays from the wild tree, swinging the gate wide for those who could stop, waving good-bys to those who must go on, and now and then offering the forlorn hope of a little bag of seeds.

Of those who gathered under his trees few had anything more palatable to eat than the dry corn dodgers and cold game of the camp. But Johnny had milk and honey, and he built a fire in his out-oven of brick and filled it with potatoes and apples to bake for the noonday meal.

It was eaten under the trees, where birds flitted about tunefully and bees wandered in the labyrinths of bloom. Then those children crusaders, safe from all alarms, went to sleep on the sun-dappled clover. The women had a social afternoon which, when they had lived long, marooned on islands of clearings twenty miles from a neighbor across a sea of trees, became historic in their memories. With the going down of the sun these pathetic guests would be gone, Johnny reflected, but he would be here to-morrow and the next year, in this safe little Eden.

His thoughts often ran into some such disturbing channel. He was glad to have them interrupted now by a farmer who hailed him from the Allegheny. Running down the grassy terraces above the town, he held the nose of the boat while the man talked. Would Johnny take a note for trees set out in the fall? He had meant to pay for them, but he had not got enough money for a boat-load of potatoes to buy a bushel of New York State salt for his cattle.

Such were the difficulties of transportation over the mountains, and the scarcity of money in Pittsburg, that produce went begging, and farmers who lived in rude abundance could not pay their debts. Johnny took the note of this honest man to save his pride, and put it into a wallet with a sheaf of other notes that were as little likely ever to be paid, or to be pressed for payment. He wrung the man's hand, shoved the boat into the current, and flung himself on the sloping bank, his thoughts thrust back into the flood of self-questioning by the farmer's last remark:

"Men out my way are feeding their left-over apples to the hogs."

Apples, too, were a drug in the market of Pittsburg. Quantities of them were turned into cider, fed to stock, or left to rot on the ground, while a hundred miles to the west they were as unobtainable as though they grew on another planet.

Johnny turned and lay with his face on his arms. Because it was unsafe and unprofitable for a nurseryman to venture to serve the wilderness, must a generation of brave men, wistful women and defrauded children miss the comfort and beauty and fond memories of orchards?

The letters that had come back to him!— letters written on wrapping-paper, on birch bark, on the fly-leaves of precious Bibles and spelling-books; letters posted in hollow trees for hunters, traders, and friendly Indians to find and carry on; letters weeks on the way, and sent with the postage for Johnny to pay out of the always scanty supply of coins in his pocket!

The people who wrote asked nothing more of him; but, very certain that he would care, they wanted to tell Johnny of the disasters that had overtaken his gifts. Young trees had died or had been swept away in fording streams. Seeds had been lost, mildewed by damp, or planted in improper soils. Plants that had sprouted had been killed by drought, choked by weeds, browsed by deer or cattle, or burned by the Indians in their annual firing of underbrush. How could it be otherwise where men must fell trees, raise cabins, grub stumps, plow corn, fence out wild beasts and hunt against famine?

In time the wilderness must give way before the souls of such dauntless men. But it would yield to nothing less. It rejected Johnny's gifts of tender seeds and trees long cherished. It would always refuse them unless—he gave himself to their defense.

As clear as the bugles that began to blow, to announce that the boats were going out,

Johnny heard that voiceless call to go and plant orchards in the wilds. He had no ties or duties to hold him here; no work that a man much older than himself could not do as well.

But could he give up all the days of his youth—his dream of love and home? In such a lifelong wandering he could not have a cabin and a family. He must sow in solitude, and see his harvests gathered to cheer the firesides of other men. He could have no love but that of mankind, no children besides the tender seeds of his planting. And at the end he must come to some death obscure and lonely.

He could not do it.

Very certain of that he got to his feet, shaken by the spiritual struggle. His guests were already in the bustle and excitement of hurried departure, and there was no time for lingering good-bys or backward looks. Hastily loading them with fruit and blossoms, he helped the smallest children down the steep hill to the town.

There every able-bodied man was needed. A string of boats had come down from yards farther up the Monongahela, and a hundred unmanageable craft were all in a tangle on the current that was running five miles an hour. There was a pandemonium of shouts and screams from water-washed decks, and from the banks that were crowded with spectators, as collisions were threatened, boats grazed rocks or went aground on mud-bars.

With other men and boys Johnny raced into the flood that covered Water Street, to pull a luckless raft from under the keel of the mail-packet. Lending a hand with pole or oar or rope to boats in trouble, he made his way along shore, scrambling over picket fences of gardens that were under water. When the danger was past he mounted the outside stairs to the upper story of the little, old brick blockhouse of Fort Pitt, that still stood on the first bank above the fork of the rivers.

An Irish widow lived there in the sixteen-foot-square redoubt of Colonel Boquet, with a progeny as numerous as that of the old woman in the shoe. Children tumbled up and down the muddy steps; pigeons flew in and out of the powder-burned loopholes under the timbered eaves; and over the great pond below, which filled the approach to Duquesne Way, thousands of wild ducks made a deafening clamor. But, next to his orchard on the hill, this was the best lookout in the town. Johnny always stood there, if he could get a foothold in the press, to watch the wagons and boats go out.

For miles the caravans could be seen moving along the northern bank of the Ohio, and the fleet drifting down the flood in a rude pageantry of migration that was epic in its proportions and daring. To the depths of him it stirred Johnny. Out on that horizon of brooding woods and uncharted waters lay the task of the time, and these were the people who, with any tool or skill, crude strength or sheer courage they possessed, leaped to the doing of it. There would be small reward for these of the vanguard, no return in glory. It had the thrill of heroic adventure, the splendor of self-sacrifice, the tragic mischances of battle. Johnny burned with shame as he remembered how he had been counting the cost. While the boats went by he stood uncovered.

His earliest guests of the morning passed the fork with another family on a clumsy flatboat. The woman was leaning on the boarded-up stern, looking up to the orchard on the hillcrest. When she saw Johnny she waved a branch of apple-blossoms, and held up the little bag of seeds, to show that she still had it safe. A lurch of the raft, as it swung into the current of the Ohio, threw her off her balance. The seeds were wrenched from her hold and flung into the flood.

For a long moment she stood motionless and stared into the swirl of turbid water in the wake of the boat, in frightened disbelief that they were gone. Johnny, too, gazed at the spot where they went down, remembering what she had said in the morning:

"Nothing must happen to my seeds. I could not bear it, because—"

The pity of it! All those little promises of beautiful and fruitful years; all those happy times and memories for the child unborn, drowned in the river's slime. For a moment she gripped the rail and smiled back at Johnny her brightest and bravest, as if to reassure him that she meant to bear what she could not. But suddenly she crumpled up on the deck and flung her arms out in piteous appeal.

It was a prayer! Countless backward looks and letters were translated. For five years the wilderness had been flinging his futile gifts in his face and besieging his spirit with prayer.

SHE HELD UP THE LITTLE BAG OF SEEDS, TO SHOW THAT SHE STILL HAD IT SAFE

Above the noises on the river he could not make her hear a consoling word even if, in his confusion, he could find one to say; but he stood there with bent head until the sun, too, dropped into the flood and the boats disappeared in the twilight behind the islands.

Hill-slope and orchard lay in the radiance of a high moon when Johnny went up through the town. As he opened the cabin door the silvery light filled the dear, familiar home and the breeze set the little chair into a ghostly rocking. A gust of emotion swept over him. But after a moment he stopped the chair, as one closes the eyes of the beloved dead, and put it back against the wall where it could rock no more.

All night he lay on the bench in the sapling stoop, like one of his own trees uprooted. The birds sang their mating songs in a dawn of rose and pearl. Then the orchard was a surf of bloom that, to Johnny's enlarged spiritual vision, had a rarer loveliness than that of color and perfume.

Apple-blossoms were the year's first assurance of a fruitful autumn, and men were as trees walking. His gift for planting and nurturing, his poetic feeling, his fellowship for men and his yearning desire to serve them, had been nothing more than the brief blush and fragrance of the wild tree that ripened only to a harvest of bitter disappointment.

God helping him, he would bring these blossoms of his soul to the good fruits of a thousand orchards in the wilderness.

3

II

THE WILDERNESS TRAIL

AD his fields been in corn,
Johnny could have sold or abandoned them and journeyed westward on the crest of that ex-
alted mood. But with a nursery
a man must keep faith from sea-
son to season, and hold his plantation in trust
for the community he serves. He could not
sell to the first or highest bidder, but only
to the man who was best fitted to continue
his work in Pittsburg. Then he had to tarry
until autumn for the ripening of seeds; spend
the winter in gleaning them at scattered farm
cider-mills, and delay his going until the
frost was coming out of the ground. But the
orchardist must know how to wait, for other
sowers reap ten times before he gathers his
first harvest. Blossom-time had almost come

24

'round again before Johnny was off on his lifelong mission in the wilderness.

It was not until fall that he parted with his little Eden for a sum that would barely outfit him for travel—that would buy him a good horse and saddle, leather saddle-bags to hold safe and dry quite a bushel of apple-seeds, a blanket and a rifle. Of food he meant to carry only a small bag of meal and a lump of salt. Gun and fishing-tackle must supply his needs. For the rest, he had the light hoe, rake and hatchet that had grown to his hand, a coil of rope and a hunting-knife. Flint and steel for fire-building were in his pouch with his Bible and the small sum of money that he had collected on his notes.

About money Johnny was in no way concerned. It would be of less use to him than courage and resource, and the co-operation and faith of the many people, both around Pittsburg and in Ohio, to whom he must look for help. Seeds were his first necessity— seeds in quantity limited only by his ability to gather, carry and plant them, and for as many years as the West might require to grow its own supply.

The task he had set himself was appalling,

but the result was assured. He had but to sow a hundred seeds for one to survive to the transplanting; set out ten trees to bring one to the age of bearing, and grow an uncertain number of those to secure one of value. Most of his seedling trees, he knew, would revert to their wild ancestry. Only now and then would one come true to its variety or develop some rare perfection of its own. And budding and grafting must long be as impossible in the backwoods as they were for the Pilgrims of the *Mayflower*. But it was thus that, in spite of stony ground, bitter climate and Indian wars, orchards blushed and fruited within a generation in every colony of New England. The West must reward his devotion much more quickly and generously.

Since the best investment he could make of his walletful of notes was to put them into men's good-will, Johnny tucked them under the front logs of glowing fireplaces before the eyes of the poor farmers who had given them. And to men who protested that they still owed him, he said:

"You owe orchards to pioneers in the backwoods. Let me collect the debt in seeds and in a winter night's lodging now and then for the next twenty years or so."

With that he went whistling to the heap of fermenting or frozen pomace with an iron soap-kettle of warm water to wash out the seeds. There, in an open pole shack or under the bare trees, he worked in wind or rain, snow or bitter cold. At nightfall he brought in a small measure of sorted seed, for he saved only the brightest and plumpest, and spread them on the chimney-shelf to dry.

One place exhausted, he shouldered his bag and tramped to the next. Now and then he lay out among the hills to harden himself to danger and exposure, or in times of spiritual stress to keep a vigil with the stars. In that first winter of wandering in the sparsely set-tled and drift-filled valleys about Pittsburg he grew lean and long of stride, and his eyes took on the look of one who sees no hard or hindering circumstance, but only the distant and splendid goal.

Except in moments of excitement, Johnny was a man of brief and diffident speech. It was only by accident that he fully revealed his unworldly and perilous scheme of life, and won the approval of more prudent friends.

In reading of the miracle of the loaves and fishes to an illiterate family, about a fire where apples sputtered in a spicy row, he had a vision of his orchard multiplied. Then his dark-gray eyes went black and luminous. Words tumbled out in one of those cataracts of eloquence with which he now and then swept away three generations of men on floods of poetic and religious feeling for his self-imposed task. Until far into the night he talked of his mission. God and one man were going to bring about that miracle, and feed the multitude in the wilderness with comfort and beauty.

At mill and store, and wherever people hailed one another on land and water highway, the story was repeated. With surprising rapidity and accuracy of report it spread over the region and touched the imagination and social conscience of all manner of men. Here was a thing to which the right thinking must lend a hand. So, even before he had started on his first journey, Johnny had become a matter of public pride and concern, a beloved figure about whom a legend had begun to grow.

But there was no one to see him off, and the world was stripped to the elements of bleak

weather, bare woods and leaden waters, on
the dark winter morning when Johnny rode
down to the ferry landing to meet the star-
route post-rider. It had been urged upon
him as safest to cover the first stage of the
journey with the mail-carrier, who, in the last
year, had been making the round trip once
a week to the new settlement of a blacksmith
shop and floating mill at Zanesville. Thence
he could drop, from one cluster of cabins to
another, down the Muskingum.

To have the longest planting season possible
he was obliged to go out thus, ahead of the
spring tide of migration, for the red maple
often blossomed late in February at Marietta,
and the Judas-tree in March. By traveling
fast and working his way on the flatboats of
home-seekers, and on the freight-pirogues that
carried salt and gunpowder to the remotest
clearings on the larger tributaries, he could
put in seeds near most of the white settlements in Ohio. The red tribes still held the
Northwest and, in winter, ranged their ancient hunting-grounds in the eastern foot-hills
within a day's ride out of Pittsburg.

During the summer, when no planting could
be done, Johnny meant to search out scat-

tered clearings along the smaller waterways and trails to the Indian border. In October and November he would put in what seeds he had left along the route of his return for a new supply. The winter months he must spend among the cider-mills, and late February must see him on the wilderness trail. Until there were orchards in the new West he might not see blossoming or fruiting apple-trees again.

There had been a thaw and then a freeze. Gales had swept the hilltops bare, but snow still lay in the forest and in shrinking patches in the hollows. Once across the Allegheny, where the ferry nosed its way through floating ice and muddy slush, the rough-shod horses picked their way over the iron ruts and around the shivering pools of the Great Trail.

The cutting of this military road through a hundred miles of unbroken woods, for a forced march of kilted Highlanders to the meadows of the Muskingum, was a wonder tale of the breaking of the power of Pontiac. Unused for thirty years and obliterated by new growth, it had been reopened, after Wayne's victory in 1794, by a peaceful army of home-seekers only five years before Johnny began his mission. It was still, with the exception of the larger waterways, the only way of travel in the forests west of Pittsburg of which eagles were aware.

To the mouth of Beaver Creek it defiled along the north bank of the river. There the Ohio dropped away to the south, while the road ran westward along the watershed. Travel over it was nearly all in one direction. Its only purpose was to cleave a way to the first navigable stream in the heart of a wilderness that had engulfed forty thousand unreturning pioneers. There were no settlements or even isolated cabins along this road that was walled by wild flood and gigantic trees. No alien sound was heard by the travelers besides the occasional crack of the red man's rifle in the hills.

All day the horses scrambled up and down the rough ridges; plunged into the black mold and dense thickets of tangled gullies; stumbled around splintered and root-buttressed stumps; struggled across corduroyed bogs; raced trembling over thawing quicksands, and splashed through creeks that foamed and chuckled under the marble-white arches of leafless sycamores. Fording-places were uncertain, for after every freshet mud-bars shifted up or down stream. When one could not be found the crossing had to be made at a riffle, often with a precipitous approach, where the horses were in danger of pitching their riders headlong or of breaking their own legs.

At nightfall the travelers camped in one of those oases of the forest—a natural "opening" that sloped to a creek-bank and was girdled by tall trees. The horses were belled and turned loose to feed on the scant growth of grass and buffalo clover that had sprung up in the late thaw. Then, while the post-rider went hunting, Johnny built a fire of driftwood and found a dry cache for the mail and seed bags in a hollow tree. It was a half-hour after the report of the gun before the man returned to camp with a brace of venison steaks and the freshly flayed skin of a buck.

"You killed a deer to make a meal for two men?" asked Johnny. He was willing to take what life he must to sustain his own, but he hated to see any living thing destroyed needlessly, or any useful thing wasted.

The mail-carrier laughed and slapped his thigh in huge enjoyment. "Say, Johnny, didn't you know it was a public duty to make game scarce along this road? Travel will be safer when them thieving redskins are obliged to leave this neck of the woods. Yep, there'll be trouble, you bet. Indians always fight before they move west." He lit his pipe and considered Johnny with affectionate concern. "See here, Johnny, you don't want to have anything to do with them red devils."

Johnny said nothing, but he could not eat of the venison. He caught a fish in the creek and baked a hoe-cake. Long after the other man slept he lay thinking how he and his mission were involved in the wrongs and hostilities that had imperiled life and work on every American frontier. And when he was awakened in the night by the snarling of wolves over the dead buck, this wild way over which he must journey year after year became a place of pitiless betrayal of peaceful things that asked only to go about their business unmolested. This year's leaves might well drift over him, and he and his dream of service to his generation lie slain and forgotten on the leaf-mold, the ancient death-bed of the woods.

In the morning his horse was gone. The

bell and the shapeless prints of moccasined feet were found in the wet moss of that charming glade, where the first venturesome robin hopped and chirped in the pale winter sunshine. This was a calamity that he had not foreseen.

The mail-carrier was in one of those flaming rages of retaliation that, in white men and red, have started every border war. "It's murder to steal a man's horse in these woods. If it was mine I'd get it back if I had to follow the dirty thief to his village at Sandusky or Piqua and fill his copper-colored hide with buckshot."

"I have no quarrel with any man," said Johnny.

"O Lord!" He shrugged his shoulders in disgust. "The first time you get a shot from behind a tree you'll change your mind about that. Well, camp here. I'll be back in four days. We'll cache all the plunder but the mail, and you can ride double with me to Pittsburg and get another horse."

Johnny could not consider this. "My seeds would mildew if they were buried a week or so. And I haven't enough money to buy a horse."

"Then you'll have to wait for a caravan to pick you up. The first emigrants will be along in a couple of weeks."

"I must be in Marietta by that time. Good-by, and better luck to you."

"You talk like a fool!" The man leaped to the saddle angrily, mounted to the trail, and rode away. The United States mail could not be delayed; and he reflected that, with a horse-load of baggage, Johnny had no choice but to stay where he was. But a mile up the road he recalled the something in Johnny's look that had alarmed him, and came pounding back.

"Johnny, you've got to camp here. There are more Indians farther west. I didn't know there was a redskin near here, or I wouldn't 'a' killed that buck. I done you a bad turn."

Johnny looked up at him with a glow of warm feeling as he remembered the many stories of this man's bravery, resourcefulness and faithfulness to duty. In spite of storm and flood, accidents to horses, treachery of Indians and encounters with wild animals, he had always brought the mail-bag through.

"Then you'll do me a good turn and take my seeds to Zanesville. You know Isaac

Stadden, the German farmer who went out
from Pittsburg last year. His clearing is near
the mouth of the Licking River. Leave the
saddle-bags with him, and tell him I will be
there within a week to plant the first nursery
in the Northwest Territory on his farm."

The man went white. "Why, good Heavens, Johnny, this road kills horses! There are
wolf-packs, and the first band of Indians you
met would strip you to your shirt and lose
you in the woods."

"I'll get through somehow. Good - by!"
There was in Johnny's look the pale exaltation of the fanatic who is not to be turned
from his purpose. He smiled and waved his
coonskin cap as long as the slowly departing
rider was in view.

He had begun to make a drag-litter which
he could pull, after the manner of an Indian
pony, and use to raft his baggage across
streams. But now, lightened of his seeds,
he made up his tools, his food-pouch and his
blanket into a compact bundle with the rope.
Shouldering his gun and his pack, he climbed
to the trail.

All day he toiled up innumerable ridges,
and then ran down, for this foot-hill country

of the Alleghanies was a storm-furrowed and petrified ocean. The road that labored up to rocky crests and dropped into sodden wallows of troughs, was one upon which a seasoned saddle-horse could not safely be driven more than thirty miles a day. Indians crossed it in many places, but they never traveled on it for any distance. They followed the easier grades of the old north and south hunting-trails that wound along the bluffs. Yet from late dawn until early dusk Johnny walked, with brief pauses for rest on hilltops. How many days he could keep up this pace he did not permit himself to think. His feet winged with purpose he had, as yet, little sense of fatigue.

But he went warily, for the way was one of pitfalls, and to a man alone and afoot the difficult miles were ambushed. In that colossal forest the rough-hewn road was but a rift, a crevice between cliffs of trees, and fifty yards on either side every columned vista ended in gloom. The crack of rifles became louder and more frequent. Stretches of soft earth showed the tracks of animals, large and small. The wayside was strewn with the skulls and scattered bones of horses and cattle which, having strayed or been injured, had been abandoned by hurrying emigrants. There were mounds with rude headboards. One had been torn open—a gash in the soft bosom of mother earth. Johnny stopped to draw a covering of soil into the trench and to say a prayer.

He was afraid of but two things—of being molested and delayed by man or beast, and of losing the trail. Once he slipped farther into a thicket than he had intended while a band of Indian hunters went by overhead, and in coming out again he lost his sense of direction. It was a half-hour before, through a maze of brush-grown glens, he found his way back to the road.

At night he made his camp in a little cave on a steep slope twenty feet below the trail. From the quantity of small bones in it and the vile smell, it was probably an old fox-den. He raked the refuse out, cut a hole for the escape of smoke, and sweetened the air with fire. As noiselessly as any foraging and defenseless animal he slipped about, catching a fish in a pool of the creek below, and setting loop-traps in a rabbit-run. When he had eaten his supper he put out the fire and spread his blanket. On either side the entrance, which was concealed by bushes, he drove stout stakes and wove his rope across. Then he knotted a kerchief to the screen. As long as the faint moonlight penetrated the leafless web of the forest it would flutter there, a pale flame that would make prowling animals pause.

In spite of the pain in his bruised and swollen feet and legs, and such cramped quarters that he could not stretch at full length, Johnny fell, almost at once, into the sleep of exhaustion. It was toward morning, when the wind went down with the moon, that he woke with a start in darkness and silence and to the fetid breath of a wolf. At the hissing flash and acrid smoke of a little train of gunpowder that he fired with flint and steel, the creature fled, crashing through undergrowth. Overhead a panther screamed and leaped away across the tree-tops.

Johnny slept no more. For that night he was safe enough, but a cave was not always to be found. A fire in the open was a man's natural home in the woods, and a rifle his defense. But the glow of flames or the sound of a shot here might summon the Indians, and them he must avoid until opportunity offered to commend himself. Now and then a white man—a trapper with a wild strain in him, a trader with a finer sense of fair play, or a missionary with only the love of God and the brotherhood of man in his heart, did make his own terms of peace with them. He must do that, be able to join their bands of hunters for safe travel, be welcome in their camps, turn this peril into a protection, or see his mission perish.

Dawn came in as a diffused light, cold and gray. After an hour on the road Johnny was obliged to take shelter in the burned-out hollow of an enormous tree, while a smother of soft snow blotted out the world. The storm died away to a drizzling rain that veiled the woods and mired the road. At every step his clogged feet slipped. At the bottom of every ravine ran a swollen creek where he had to put his pack, his gun and his clothing on his head and wade in icy water, sometimes plunging into sink-holes up to his shoulders.

It was mid-afternoon when he came to a broader stream that poured down a torrent of mud, melting snow and driftwood. He could not swim it with his baggage, and any

raft that he could build and man would be
swept away. Up-stream he scrambled, along
steep and crumbling banks, to where the
channel narrowed so that the limbs of sycamores were interlaced above a foaming riffle.
Pulling his pack up into a tree, he swung it at
the end of the rope like a pendulum and landed
it on the farther bank. Then he leaped,
caught a branch that broke under his weight,
fell ten feet to another, and hung there until
he could make his way to the ground. Through
two miles of tangled bog he struggled back to
the trail.

In rounding a bend half-way up the next long
slope, he almost ran into a timber-wolf which
was squatted on its haunches in the roadway,
muzzle up, as if keeping some ghoulish watch.
Gaunt from a hard winter, it held its ground
and showed its fangs when Johnny struck it
with a stone. He shot it as it opened its jaws
to howl for the pack; and he raced up the slippery rise in such haste to be beyond the range
of the echoing report, that he stumbled over
an Indian who had fallen on his face across
the road.

In a moment he had turned the brave on
his back, felt the faint heart-beat, shook and

shouted him into semi-consciousness, and learned his first Shawnese word from the dry lips that begged for water.

"Courage, comrade!" Johnny knew that all Indians learned enough English to keep from being cheated in the fur-trading. He asked brief questions about this man's companions and the location of his camp, but the dazed savage only stared in a bewildered way, tried to draw his knife, and muttered unintelligibly.

Blood was trickling from a gunshot wound in a leg. Johnny cut the soaked legging away, washed the ragged furrow, and made bandages of the linsey shirt that he wore under his buckskins. Then he dragged the senseless giant to the shelter of the trees, bathed his scratched and mud-stained face, and covered him with his own blanket. He found no gun near, and hastily loaded his own that had been discharged.

Every consideration of prudence urged him to run, not to become involved in this obscure tragedy. No doubt this hunter would be missed, and men of his tribe might appear at any moment. The rain had ceased and night was coming on, sharp and still. He

stood on such an elevation, which dropped
away so steeply that he could look out over

'COURAGE, COMRADE!" BUT THE DAZED SAVAGE TRIED TO
DRAW HIS KNIFE

gray billows of tree-tops to purple banks of sunset.

There he built a great fire—a beacon that shone across the heaving ocean of woods. At intervals he fired his rifle to guide the searchers. Making a hasty meal of the parched corn and jerked venison in the Indian's pouch, he hurried to gather fuel for the night. Then he cut two poles from sassafras saplings, and a quantity of brush and slender grape-vines as flexible as ropes. These he spent the early hours of the night in weaving into a litter, so there would be no delay or discomfort in getting the wounded man to camp. It was near midnight when three Indians with pine-knot torches and bristling with weapons, slipped like apparitions out of the forest. Johnny stood up, unarmed, and met their dark looks with candor and sympathy.

"Your brother lives. He knew nothing when I found him here, but may be able to tell you about his mishap in the morning. I would not wake him now. He has lost much blood and is in a fevered sleep."

Johnny turned from them to test the strength of the litter. Without taking their

44

eyes from him, they went to look at the sleeping brave and to inspect the neat bandages. Then they drew their blankets about them and lay down by the fire. Johnny read a chapter in his Bible by the flare, said good night, and stretched himself beside the wounded man to share the covering. If this injured hunter could give no account of himself in the morning, or if he mistook Johnny for his assailant, there might be a swift reckoning. But he would not think of that. He was so exhausted by the day's march and the night's anxious watch that he was sound asleep in five minutes.

He woke with such stiff and aching limbs that the thought of the wild leagues that lay before him filled him with sick misgivings. The Indians already had their injured tribesman on the litter and they had his story. He had shot himself accidentally when he slipped in the mud and tripped over washed-out roots, a mile back on the bluff trail, and had dragged himself to the road. They had found his gun where he had dropped it in the path, and the dead wolf on the slope. But for this white wayfarer the bones of this young warrior would have been stripped, and wolves did not wait until a helpless man was dead.

"All men should be brothers in these woods," said Johnny.

The Indians were silent, but they shared their food with him, and watched curiously as he hobbled about. They had been so taken up with their own trouble that they had not speculated on his presence there alone, in the heart of the wilderness. But now they noticed his lameness and his torn and mired boots, and one asked, bluntly:

"Where is your horse?"

"I had a horse." Johnny's level look was fearless, but it did not accuse them. It was, indeed, full of infinite understanding and compassion. "Let us say no more about that." He held out his hand in friendly parting and began to tie up his pack.

They made haste to say that they knew nothing about his horse, but they would keep a lookout for the thief. And word of how he had stood by this wounded brave should go over every trail of the forest. No Shawnee would ever rob him again. And if he would follow them to their camp they would see him safe to his journey's end.

Johnny's heart leaped in his breast. "Will you lend me a pony and a guide to the Great Crossing, and a canoe to Marietta?"

"Come!" They took up the litter and turned into the bluff trail. Without an instant's hesitation Johnny shouldered his gun and his pack and followed these Ishmaels of the forest whose tribal name was a synonym for restless wandering, for ferocity and treachery. The foot-path worn deep in the soil, the undergrowth arching overhead, the narrow trace was no more than a human rabbit-run in the woods.

Two days later he was set afloat in a beautiful painted canoe on the winding current of the Muskingum. Paddling swiftly down to Zanesville, he left the mill, the stockade, and scattered cabins behind, after shouting to the blacksmith that he would return, and upon what errand. It was near sundown when he breasted the spring-flood sweep of the Licking.

The wild geese were coming north. Frogs piped in the swamps. Does were bringing their spotted fawns down to drink. The ice was all out, and streams were bank-full from melting snow. Sap was running, and squaws were boiling sugar in the maple groves. Miasmic vapors rose from the marshes. Up all the foot-hill valleys of the western slope spring was hurrying, as if on the wings of song. The black soil of the Ohio bottoms was warming for Johnny's seeds. The river, lying in the track of the sun, was a stream of glory when he beached his canoe, climbed the rail fence and ran across a clearing that was a mere window on the sky, to Isaac Stadden's cabin.

III

GOOD SAMARITANS

DOWN the Muskingum Johnny dropped so rapidly, stopping only for a day or two at each cluster of cabins to put in a small nursery, that he ran ahead of rumor. Below Big Bottom and Fort Frye the current slackened, and his approach to Marietta was indicated when the stream widened to two hundred yards and the spectral sycamores that marched with its banks were no longer able to meet in high arches overhead. But even there he was still in the wilds, his water highway girt by steep hills, hemmed in by tall timber, and fed by countless little singing creeks. A clearing at which he asked permission to use any bit of waste land suitable for his purpose, and the pleasant tinkle of cow-bells in the woods, were signs that he was on the outskirts of the dauntless town which, only a dozen years before, had been the first to front the flood of the River Beautiful.

Then there were sounds of hammers, the zipping wail of a saw in hard wood, and the clatter of a fallen plank that sent birds and squirrels skurrying to cover. Another man in his place, after three weeks in the wilderness, would have dipped the paddle briskly to round the next bend where, no doubt, lay a floating mill, and some such ambitious and social business as putting proper floors and doors in a cabin was afoot. But Johnny nosed his canoe into a clump of willows on the eastern bank, jumped out, and broke through the tasseling screen into a hill and tree-rimmed cove.

It was just such a place as he looked for everywhere—a sheltered nook overgrown with all the flowering vines and shrubs of the forest. To lovely and neglected spots like this songbirds retreated before the devastation of white men, and later generations of children found the thorny thickets of wild-apple blossoms that were a beautiful by-product of Johnny's labors. Not large enough for fields, too steeply walled for safe pastures, they were long left undisturbed to the slow-growing seeds of his planting.

Johnny lost no time in getting to work. From soil as soft and loose as an ash-heap he pulled forest seedlings and weed-stalks by hand. Tough bushes, briers and saplings he cut down with his hatchet, and grubbed out the roots; and with his hoe he destroyed the innumerable cones of annuals that, pushing through the blanket of drifted leaves, ran up every rise in flickers of pale-green fire. The ground cleared over a fraction of an acre on the well-drained slope that faced westward toward the river, he raked it free of clods, opened orderly rows of trenches, and put in and covered up his seeds.

He was used to working thus all day, often eating a noon snack of rude fare on his feet, and not stopping until he had marked the plot and closed any opening in the protecting wall with a stout barrier of stakes and brush. But for several nights now, whether in the open or on a cabin hearth, he had slept ill and had wakened shivering in the cold dawns when fog sheeted the marshy bottom-lands. In the middle of the afternoon he cooled his

hot face and hands at a spring and lay down
on a patch of buffalo clover.

Scarcely a murmur of the world without
penetrated the little greening hollow that
distilled the earliest incense of spring. The
sounds of tools, so loud on the river, were soft-
ened here to the drumming of woodpeckers,
chattering of squirrels and songs of birds.
In his swift travel, where he bespoke men
only in passing, Johnny was coming to find
companionship in his furred and feathered
neighbors, noting their nest-building, courtship-caroling, and busy foraging. His glance,
roving up to a crow that cawed from the top
of a cottonwood, fell to a fluttering patch of
the discreetly warm color of the tea-roses that
had bloomed beside his grandmother's cot-
tage door in Boston. Then there was a laugh
that bubbled up from the heart of a child.

"Oh! I thought you were an Indian!"

Johnny scrambled to his moccasined feet,
for he had discarded his torturing boots in
the Shawnee camp, and took off his fur
cap to the little maid above him. Her full-
skirted gown of linsey, that blew in the breeze
about her ankles, and the folded kerchief,
were of a fashion that went out when the un-

happy queen for whom Marietta was named
laid her lovely head on the block. The color
of the gown was but temporary—a spring
blossoming, as it were, due to experimental
steeping in sassafras tea.

"There are no Indians about here," Johnny
reassured her, gravely; but she nodded posi-
tively.

"They always come down the bluff trail
along the west bank to sell their furs when
the geese fly north." She seated herself on
the buttressing roots of a beech-tree, on the
rim of his horizon, and took her knitting
from her belt. Girls were obliged to grow up
early in that day and place. At sixteen most
of them were married, and idleness was sin
in a maid of fourteen.

"I'm as 'fraid as death of Indians." She suddenly turned a pallid face and wide blue eyes
upon him—a look that he remembered, when
he saw it again in tortured fancy years afterward in an hour of anguish. "They—they
killed—my father and mother—in the massacre—at Big Bottom."

Johnny bared his head. Big Bottom, forty
miles up the Muskingum, was now a place
of corn and wheat fields, of grazing cattle and

populous cabins. It had been difficult for him to realize the tragic event there of ten years before, that had ushered in half a decade of savage warfare. Such horrors might happen again; there was a stockade in every settlement, and the government's Fort Harmer at Marietta. But presently she put the matter out of her mind, showing of what sterling New England stuff she was fashioned.

"I came to find these hepaticas, and to sit by them awhile."

She cleared last year's rusty foliage from a nest of faint-blue blossoms, and then, blushing a little, kissed them and left them to nod on their mossy stems. A Puritan maid, she was far too well brought up to ask questions, but she glanced curiously at the small, cultivated plot, and Johnny held up a handful of shining brown seeds.

"I know what they are—apple-seeds! Dr. True has an apple-tree, and when it blooms it's the wonder of the town. The older people tell fairy-stories of orchards in the East that bury little homes in blossoms. I wish—"

She stopped, for Johnny had flung his arm across his eyes. After a moment he looked at her again. "There will be such orchards

here for every one." His face was so pale,
but his smile so grave and sweet, that she fell
into a wondering silence. She was not surprised to find him here, for in this Mecca
of the New West strangers arrived by every
boat and over every trail of the forest; but
it was an unheard-of thing to see a man
planting trees where every other one was at
the bitter necessity of chopping them down.
By and by she remembered a polite ceremony
that had been omitted.

"My name is Betty Stacey. Please, will
you tell me yours?"

"Johnny."

It occurred to neither of them that the in-
formation lacked anything, and now that they
were acquainted she offered shy confidences
and hospitality.

"It was Aunt Mary Lake who found me
where mother hid me in the woods, and
brought me up. She isn't any relation, but
just everybody's Aunt Mary. She must be
getting old, for she's sixty; but she's so busy
doing things for people that I guess she forgot about it. Won't you come to see her?
Please, Johnny."

"To-morrow." He explained that he had

to make a brush fence across the gully that had been cut in the rim of the cove by the spring, to keep deer and cattle out. Then he must find some one in the town to keep weeds and forest seedlings from choking his nursery.

Betty listened with eager sympathy. Her pretty face had warmed to the blush of the wild rose, and no fox-squirrel had fur of so bright and burnished a brown as the hair that curled on her neck. It was the color that went with black-lashed eyes as darkly blue as the waters of the Muskingum, and sun-kisses across the bridge of a proud little nose that drooped at the tip.

She had meant to go, but Johnny closed his eyes as if in weariness and discomfort, and fell into such an uneasy sleep on the slope below her that she sat as still as any mouse and watched over him with sweet, maternal solicitude. The sun was shining on a level along the forest aisles when he was awakened by a crash that shook the hill. Betty was on her feet, back toward him, gazing down into the wood.

"Did the cabin fall?" he cried.

"The cabin? It was in the shipyard. A

56

prop gave way and a pile of timbers tumbled down."

He ran up the slope. Below, on a shadowy bend of the river, a wide swath had been cut in the ranks of trees, and on the grassy ways lay a long hull, like a viking ship of old on a Norse fjord. It was an astonishing thing to see an ocean-sailing vessel of a hundred tons burden nearing its launching on this far-inland stream; but Johnny remembered that the leaders of the Ohio Company were Revolutionary officers from the ports of New England, who had built a second *Mayflower* at Pittsburg. Ship-building was a habit with men of that breed, and the navigation of uncharted waters a trade.

"There," said Betty, delightedly, as a huge young negro shouldered his way through the crowd of men in the yard. "Kitt Putnam has come from the mill to pile the timbers up again. He's the biggest, strongest, kindest darky in the world. He'll keep the weeds out of your little bits of baby apple-trees for you."

Down the hill she sped in happy excitement and crossed a freshly plowed stump-lot. Johnny called to her to wait for him when she paused on the edge of a drainage ditch, looking down ruefully at her pretty, yellow moccasins, but Kitt ran and set her across. He was not a river negro from Kentucky, but a freedman who had been the body-servant of old Gen. Israel Putnam in the East. Brought out by Colonel Israel, he was a universal favorite in Marietta and Belpré because of his good manners, his prowess in sports, and the cheerful willingness with which he served every one with his phenomenal strength and dexterity.

Before she disappeared in the thin belt of forest that hid the town, the gay and tender child turned and waved to him again. Already ties of interest and affection were beginning to bind Johnny to the New West. He was no hermit of the woods. It was the pathos of his solitary and wandering life that people touched his imagination and twined about his heart.

Twilight was darkening in the cove when he came up from the deserted shipyard with fuel for his fire. For easier carriage the seeds had been transferred to a bag made of canvas from a caravan cover. With them he shared his brush bed and a corner of his blanket to protect them from the damp. Unable to eat anything, he lay down at once under a canopy of unfurling leaves so sketchy that he could consider the heavens. He knew only the polar stars, by which mariners and hunters have steered their way since time began, but he was beginning to take note of other groups and planets that bloomed nightly on the dark. And it was by such reverent and poetic watchers that the sky was mapped and peopled.

Even in his dreaming dozes Johnny was conscious of throbbing head and burning skin. Twice he got up to replenish the fire; and in a dawn turned suddenly bleak he was aroused by the desolate cries of geese winging their way northward. Then he fell into a profound sleep, and while he slept the fire was quenched by rising vapors. Fog filled the green bowl to the brim, and he woke in a chill that gripped his heart.

When the sun rose and pulled the earth cloud up into the blue, and all the undergrowth sparkled and dripped as with rain, he wrapped his blanket about the seeds and dragged himself to the sunniest slope. There he lay in a frozen agony that was unbelievable.

Soon waves of warmth ran over him, then flashes of heat, then consuming fires. Hearing the sounds of saws and hammers in the shipyard, he cried aloud for water, but could not make himself heard. He found the spring and, having drunk, fell in the cold, saturated moss and slept away the fever. It was in the white void of fog that he woke again, in a chill that was like the rigor of death.

With the return of the fever his mind wandered, so that he babbled of senseless things. But even then subconsciousness was in the grip of dark anxiety for what he must guard with his life. He groped his way blindly and flung his arms wide across the bag of seeds. Hours later he was dimly conscious of light, flying footsteps, a pulsing pillow under his head, and warm drops on his face. Then great arms lifted him into the canoe and he drifted down into darkness and oblivion.

Betty had run on before, and Mary Lake had her one four-poster bed out from the wall and spread with tow-linen sheets, when Kitt Putnam "toted" Johnny up from the river and into her good house within Marietta's old garrison inclosure of Campus Martius. When she had stripped off his wet buckskins and got him into one of her own long gowns, he lay in a restless moaning that was a piteous thing to see and hear.

Mary Lake's clear, gray eyes had seen a variety of things in many ports of the world in the forty-odd years since Captain Lake of a Newfoundland fishing fleet shipped a bride at Bristol, England. For one thing, as a nurse in Washington's camp at Fishkill, she had seen young men as ill of remittent fever as Johnny get well. The first thing to do was to have as few people underfoot as possible; so when Kitt had gone for Dr. True she shut her door against anxious and willing neighbors and pulled the latch - string in. Then she spoke to the grief and terror stricken child who clung to the foot-rail of Johnny's bed.

"Sit by him, my lass, if it will comfort 'ee, and fan him with a turkey wing." She still had a bit of her girlhood dialect, and she might have been born in her straight gray gown and snowy cap. Without haste or noise or litter, she was making papery medicine wafers in a camp spider at the huge stone fireplace when Dr. True came in.

"Oh, doctor," faltered Betty, "I think he wants water." Tears hung on her eyelashes, for even the children of that day knew that water was poison to one sick of a fever. But Dr. True was a medical heretic. And, indeed, he had been chosen by the Ohio Company to care for the health of this frontier settlement, where orthodox remedies were often not to be had, just because of his ability and willingness to lean back hard on Mother Nature and Mary Lake.

"Wants water, does he? That's reasonable. Give me such a temperature and I'd jump into the garrison well."

Johnny drank and drank and drank. The doctor flung the covers back impatiently and bade Kitt open the "port-holes," his humorous name for the small, hinged windows which were sunk in the walls of six-inch-thick, whip-sawed poplar planks. Later houses were much ruder, but the very first ones built in Marietta were dove-tailed together like the drawers of a wardrobe chest, and had proper fittings of glass and hardware.

"There, that's better. The man was gasping like a fish. Hm—hm! this is quite a conflagration. I happen to be out of that—

Guess we'll have to put this fire out with water, Mary."

Betty was set to washing Johnny's earth-stained face and hands while Mary Lake bathed the burning body under the sheet. The doctor asked no questions about his patient, for he was at the free call of every stranger within the gates; and Mary Lake's house was a hospital, in time of need, maintained by the Ohio Company. But the young face on the pillow interested and puzzled him, for it was of a type not often seen in the ruthless business of pioneering. An Ichabod Crane of a middle-aged bachelor, he sat with one long, thin leg dangling over the other, peering around his big nose with the one eye that was of any use to him, and switching back the hair that he still wore in a ribboned cue, in the inconvenient fashion of an earlier day.

By the dim light of deer-tallow candles the two toiled over Johnny. The doctor kept a finger on the small, hard, racing pulse, and three times during the night-watch he gave a dose of some remedy which he managed never to be without.

"He's holding his own—the heart rallies."

The medicine-man looked encouragement across to his white-haired comrade of many a victory over death since they two lifted the siege of smallpox from this garrison, in the first, hard year of occupation. They were still toiling when a cock crew.

"The turn is coming. Be ready, Mary. We shall have to be getting this man warm, soon."

The opening of Mary Lake's door was a signal for help, and the giving of it a public duty. Night-capped heads looked out of half the twenty plank houses that faced one another from the four sides of the square.

"Boil corn, and keep the kettles hot against Kitt's coming. Some one milk a cow, and I'm giving my lassie leave to rob any nest of a fresh egg." She roused the negro, who had slept on a buffalo robe on the hearth. "Kitt, do 'ee get into Mr. Woodbridge's store on The Point; aye, lad, if ye have to break in, and fetch a jug of whisky."

The fever went suddenly, leaving Johnny collapsed, all but senseless, and drenched with icy sweat. Only the black knight of emergencies had the swift and easy strength to rub the warming alcohol in hard and fast enough, and then to truss the patient up into that primitive hot pack, the "corn sweat." Milk and eggs and the broth of wild ducks fed the flickering fires of life and helped break the rigors of a chill that was without tremors; and perspiration checked the rising temperature. Then the fight began again, for this severest form of malaria that struck down the imprudent new-comer along the undrained waterways of the West, ran its course in a vicious circle that gave the victim no rest.

Kitt had brought all of Johnny's belongings up from the cove; so when, in his delirium, he cried out for his seeds, Betty dragged the heavy bag to the bedside. "Here they are, Johnny, all safe," and she guided his searching hand.

"Why, what— Who's this?" The fruit and flower loving doctor, who had helped Major Doughty bring up peach - seeds with army stores from the Potomac, and plant them about Fort Harmer and in the settlement, drew out a handful of the astonishing contents of the bag. "A nurseryman!"

"He planted a big patch on Commodore Whipple's farm above the shipyard, and he said there would be orchards here for every

one, as if he meant—meant to give his little
apple-trees away."

The doctor put the precious seeds back,
and tied the string securely, so that not one
should fall on the stony ground of Mary
Lake's scoured maple floor. And when he
found the initials "J. C." rudely splashed in
butternut dye on the canvas, he dropped to
his seat.

"It's Jonathan Chapman, that good—
good Samaritan of Pittsburg, come to settle
in Marietta. Praise God, from whom all
blessings flow!"

The first things of which Johnny was clearly conscious were the hum of Betty's flax-
wheel and the pleasant vision of Mary Lake
at her loom. Then a little boy stood in the
doorway, rubbing the dusty toes of one foot
against the other ankle, and staring at a man
in bed on a sunny day.

"Do 'ee get him a cooky, my lass."

The wheel whirred to a stop, and Betty,
going to a built-in corner cupboard, took a
crisp cake from a covered jar of brown crockery. She gave it to the child with an affectionate pinch of the red cheek, and he was
gone in a flash. Afterward Johnny heard

66

the wonder-story of the cooky-jar that Mary
Lake had bought in Bristol on her wedding-
day, and kept filled with unaccustomed sweets
for the bridegroom captain and the crew of
the *Mary Bird* all the way to the Grand
Banks of Newfoundland. By miracles of resourcefulness, and a loving-kindness that had
never failed, it had been replenished for the
pleasure of a forty-year-long procession of
children of her own and other households.

Now the flax-wheel hummed again, and
by open doors spring flowed like a healing
stream through the little home of love and
peace. It was moments before the soft air
and the smell of peach-blossoms in General
Varnum's garden made Johnny realize with
a shock the mischance that had lost him
weeks of the season's sowing.

To gain strength for his journey he began
to dig and plant in the flower-beds of every
tiny front dooryard in Campus Martius, as
soon as he could crawl out into the sunshine.
By such friendly services in picket-fenced
gardens he made his way across the strag-
gling town. The houses had been hastily built
of logs and of planks from broken-up flatboats, it is true but the muddy, stump-

strewn roads were as broad and straight, and as pleasantly shaded with forest hardwoods, as any village of New England. The settlement had its classic learning from Harvard and Dartmouth, its Yankee energy and Revolutionary courage. But the South faced it across the Ohio; the red tribes were sinister neighbors on a border that they crossed at will; and from stormy France a wave had swept its human wreckage to these far shores. So Marietta was losing its down-east speech and rigid Puritan code, and getting a viewpoint and vernacular of its own.

In less than a week Johnny started, one afternoon, to walk out to Dr. True's farm, east of the town, to see the famous apple-tree. The way lay along Sacra Via, the mounting road that had been cut through dense woods to the Big Mound—earthworks of a vanished race, now dotted with the white man's neatly lettered headboards.

At this time his orchard in Pittsburg would be in bud. It was too early to expect—and then he stopped, thinking that yearning memory was playing him a trick. But in another moment he saw the small, well-cultivated farm, forest-girt, that lay up a hillside and

looked out to the broad sweep of the river
and the Virginia mountains. The symmetrical bouquet of pink and pearl was lifted above
the rustic cabin and a thrifty plantation of
young peach-trees which had dropped their
blossoms. The doctor called to him from a
tilted chair under the boughs.

"If anybody's sick, don't tell me, Johnny.
People can be ill any time, but my apple-
tree blooms but once a year."

Exhausted by the two-mile tramp, Johnny
dropped to the grass and lay looking up with
such a smile of gentle sweetness and happiness as this medical man had never seen.
He was steeping his soul in the loveliness and
promise of the tree. What orchards he could
make grow in the mild climate and virgin soil
of the New West! The doctor had bought it
of Johnny's predecessor in Pittsburg only
seven years before, and fetched it down in
the cabin of the mail-packet. New England
could not have grown it in twenty years, and
then would have toughened and dwarfed and
twisted it into some half-wild, defiant thing.
This had sprung up straight and round-headed
as a sugar maple, bright-barked as a rose cane.
A queen of beauty of a thousand generations

of gentle ancestry, it reigned over that wild landscape, and it had its court of honey-bees.

"Are the apples good?"

The doctor could scarcely contain his pride. "It is not in full bearing yet, but it's a Summer Sweeting."

"It has a more important work to do than bearing you a crop of apples. You are going to strip it, every season, of its choicest buds, so every household for miles around can have a tree of Summer Sweetings." Johnny had lifted himself to his elbow, and his cavernous eyes darkened and glowed in a face wasted by fever. "I must teach you the art of budding and grafting."

"We are all willing to work and to make sacrifices here for the common good." The tilted chair came down, and with his hands on his knees the doctor leaned forward. Rumor had overtaken this heroic and inspired youth while he lay unconscious, and if it had not Dr. True could have read his loving purpose in the eyes that burned with zeal and compassion.

"I'll take charge of your nursery here— keep an eye on Kitt's work. Young fruit-trees are like babies. They pine away and die if they are not mothered by some one who loves them. Johnny, I thought I had heard of all the ways there were to serve God." His single eye watered, and to hide his emotion he began to scold: "Don't be so foolish as to get sick again. There are not three doctors nor two Mary Lakes in Ohio. And don't try to live on locusts and wild honey. I am often obliged to go fifty miles by canoe, or on horseback, when a man lets a tree fall on him or is clawed by a wildcat, but I sleep in a cabin and eat civilized food when I can. And when I can't I camp along the upland trails as the Indians do, and not in the bottom of a fog-well. I'll make up some Peruvian-bark powders to nip malaria in the bud."

He was coming out of the house with the packet when a man ran from the woods with incoherent cries. He had brought his young wife all the way from Big Bottom in a canoe, and she was at Mary Lake's, in the terrors and pains of first childbirth.

The doctor chuckled over his own good luck in having Johnny thrown on his hospitality. "That turns you out. Mary's got another lame dog to mend, and no room for you. You'll have to live with me until you are well enough to travel."

"I'm going to-morrow. Good-by!" He got to his feet and held out his hand. When the doctor was gone he had to fight against a weakness and lassitude that dismayed him, and against an aching desire to sleep there in the scented night and in the balmy wind which blew all the way from the Gulf. The tree had a pearly radiance in the dusk when he turned his back upon it and went swiftly down to the crowded and noisy settlement.

The spring flood - tide of migration had backed up at Marietta. For a week every sort of water craft had been making fast to the trees, for the honor of being at the launching of the *St. Clair*, the first sailing-vessel on Western waters to attempt the voyage to New Orleans. Pine torches flared from boats and landings, and from the five bastions of the pentagonal fortifications of Fort Harmer, across the Muskingum. Lower Muskingum Street, the merchants' row that ran along the bank to The Point, flared with these smoking lights and swarmed with emigrants, traders, French rowers, Negro polemen and Indians.

Through this press Johnny pushed his way. He had given half his money to the doctor, who needed all he could get "to buy medicines for poor folks." Now he spent the other half. He paid the captain of the mail-packet to fetch the little rocking-chair to Mary Lake, on his next trip from Pittsburg; and he bought a basket of maple sugar of a Shawnee squaw to help keep the cooky-jar filled.

Then for hours he stood before the door of the Ohio Company's land-office, waylaying men, inquiring their destination, marking the most energetic and public-spirited, learning that many were going to Cincinnati or to the new settlements of Chillicothe and Dayton. Was he going up the Scioto and Miami to put in his nurseries?

"I am going to the Indian border, all the way from Dayton to Cleveland," he reassured them.

It was after midnight when the crowds dispersed and the torches were extinguished. At once the illimitable leagues of woods and hills and waters went black and closed in on the sleeping town. In pitch-darkness Johnny went up the steep path to Campus Martius to leave the basket of sugar on Mary Lake's door-step. Then he descended the bluff to the bank of the Muskingum. He had a key

to the boat and warehouse where his canoe
was stored. The foul odors of skins, fish refuse, tar and hemp ropes sickened him; but
he meant to sleep there, with his bag of seeds
for a pillow, and to be away at dawn.

IV

THE QUEEN OF THE FAIRY ISLAND

OHNNY got away so very early the next morning that the blue wood - smoke had not begun to curl up from the chimneys of the town. He was storing things away compactly in the canoe when Betty ran down the bluff and sat upon a rocky shelf above him. She was of that breed of New England women who, from beach and wharf and decked house-top, watch their men go down to the sea in ships, and do what weeping they must in the night - watches. Now she gave Johnny a straw hat of her own deft and patient braiding, and then sat talking to him as he worked.

"Won't you stay for the launching? Please, Johnny! Such crowds and fun! And I want you to see our Queen of the Fairy Island, Mrs. Blennerhasset. She lives in a big white palace on Isle le Beau, across from Belpré, and she's the most beautiful lady in the world. She'll ride up through the woods to-day on a black-satin horse, and wear her scarlet habit of British army cloth. Her father was General Agnew of the English army, and she's so proud of it that she wears his colors."

Johnny smiled and shook his head at the eager child. He must be off at once and make the most of the shortened season. But he meant to stop at Isle le Beau, where he was sure of quick sympathy and intelligent cooperation. The Blennerhassets, with their fabulous wealth, luxurious style of living, and the magnificent estate that they were building up on an island in the Ohio, made a tale of Arabian Nights' enchantment to the poor and struggling people of the river settlements. And they did not hold themselves aloof. The mistress of the mansion lavished on these wilds accomplishments that had graced the courts of Europe, and the master backed every forward movement. It was he who was financing this ship-building venture. With the English love for gardening and a knowledge of botany they had made a velvet lawn, imported rare flowers, trained peach and pear trees flat against sunny walls, and were experimenting with the taming of fox-grapes and the wild berries of the forest.

"Mrs. Blennerhasset just loves Aunt Mary and she hates everything mean and cruel. One day, in Muskingum Street, she struck a man across the face with her riding-whip for beating a little colored boy. Then she wiped the whip with her lace handkerchief and rode away as scornful as a queen."

"That was fine!"

"And, Johnny, she does the kindest, sweetest things that no one else can do. She's to give a May party just to amuse people. I'm to be queen. She's making me an Empire gown of India muslin and a stockinet veil that I'm to keep for my wedding-day." She blushed prettily. "You know I'm fourteen. At sixteen I shall have to marry some one"— her blue eyes clouded with trouble—"and perhaps go away back in the woods to live, and—"

She caught his look of brooding tenderness for one of those pioneer mothers, of whom life took such fearful toll in child-bearing, hardship and danger.

"Oh, I won't mind the work, and I'd love

to have a dozen little bits of babies; but there's sure to be another Indian war, and Johnny, I couldn't bear to—to leave little children as my mother left me."

"I'll look after those babies, Betty. The Indians are friendly with me," he said, with grave gentleness. She had taken in these fears with the milk from a martyred mother's breast, and they were not groundless, even now.

She watched him wistfully as he pushed off, waved to him from the bluff, and continued to wave until his canoe passed Fort Harmer and disappeared under the arching sycamores that all but hid the mouth of the Muskingum.

The River Beautiful was a silver veil, falling from some unmarked horizon in the east; but when the sun came up over the mountains it was a narrow sea that was all one wrinkled sparkle from shore to shore. The world was merry and sweet, with dancing water, high-flying clouds, and the blowing foliage of full-leafed forests. Johnny had only to use his paddle for a rudder, for the light craft floated like a cork on the current.

From the Ohio shore the land rolled up in

soft, wooded billows. For miles the water was edged with sand or pebbled beaches, and in places the forest was pushed back by alluvial bottoms. Ten miles down he passed the cluster of cabins at Stone's Landing, and from the many boats headed up-stream and the people who were riding along the edge of the woods he knew there must be clearings up the creeks. It was still in the early hours of the morning when he ran his boat up the crescent sand beach of Belpré, the very prettiest little settlement on the river.

An offshoot of Puritan Marietta, it had a French name for its wide, terraced meadow; and it was built like a French farm village— every good house of hewn timbers facing the river on a forty-rod front, and the narrow farms marching in line back and up to a forest of oaks and hickories. At the east end of the mile-long street the stockade and blockhouses of Farmers' Castle guarded the town like a baron's château, and at the west the woods ran to the river's edge, where a grove of cedars crowned a hundred-foot bluff. Johnny marked that dry lookout for a camp.

The landing for the settlement and the

crossing to the head of Isle le Beau was at the foot of the bluff. From there he saw the white, mansard-roofed mansion, its colonnaded wings curving in a wide ellipse at the top of a sloping lawn that was shaded by a score of forest trees. Fronting the near mountains and the parted flood, and flanked by all but unbroken woods, its ordered beauty was nothing less than that of a fairy palace.

The town looked to be deserted, but as Johnny was beaching the canoe a muscular man of fifty, with the fine military bearing so common in the region, came out of a house and introduced himself as Colonel Cushing with the ease of one born to the best society of New England.

"I was to leave this canoe with you for Black Arrow, a Shawnee brave who will call for it," Johnny explained.

Together they got the handsome specimen of Indian craftsmanship into the boat-house. With keen black eyes the Colonel studied this worn and shabby young man who had been intrusted with such valuable property by an Indian. It was not until Johnny asked if there was a bit of unoccupied and defensible land near by, in which he might plant a nursery for the community, that he was recognized.

"Whoop-ee! If it isn't Johnny! Excuse me if I shake your arm off. You're the best news we've heard since the treaty of

REAR VIEW OF BLENNERHASSET HOUSE

Greenville. Colonel Israel Putnam and Mr. Blennerhasset meant to kidnap you from Marietta to-day. We have plots cleared for you, here and on the island, and fenced in according to instructions from Dr. True."

81

Johnny filled his pockets with seeds, shouldered his tools, and was making off through a kitchen garden when his host overtook him with a pair of huge, cowhide boots.

"Snakes in a swamp you have to cross—big, bad rattlers and copperheads that could take bites out of a scythe. You'd better wrap your legs with marsh-grass, too. I'll blow the dinner-horn, but it's pot-luck to-day, with your humble servant for cook. The family piled into boats and on to everything with four legs, and went to the launching. Yes, I have a full quiver, God bless 'em! and a boy and a girl orphaned by the war that we are bringing up. There's always room for one or two more in a big family."

It was a dozen years before that "room for one or two more" had any personal bearing for Johnny, but he remarked now how the people here obeyed the Biblical injunction concerning the hungry and naked, the sick and the fatherless. The Colonel laughed.

"I'll get my pay out of you, Johnny, the first time I see my youngsters set their little teeth in juicy apples. The children born out here never saw an apple, and that's something you can't describe."

"No."

They exchanged a long look that held boyhood memories of gnarly old New England orchards and the winey bins of dark cellars.

Johnny went whistling up that sloping mile of mellow furrows and through a belt of woods that was honey-sweet with blossoming tuliptrees. Blackbirds skurried up from the rank growth of the swamp that was knee-deep in ooze, and blue heron swung low over acres of budding flags and lily-pads. He saw no reptiles, but while he was putting in his seeds on the drained and sheltered bank, a doe came down to a spring to drink and an Indian paddled out to open water to shoot ducks. In the five years since the close of the war the river settlements had not been able to push back the wilderness more than two miles.

After dinner Johnny started to return to Stone's Landing. He had scarcely passed beneath the shadow of the forest when he heard a piteous whinnying from the wayside. A horse lay there in the undergrowth, his head in a little space of cropped clover.

By dint of much encouragement Johnny got the animal to his feet and down the bank into the water. But after the horse had drunk he stood so drooping and trembling, lifting one foot after the other, that Johnny, fearing he might fall and drown, got him back to the sand. Help was needed, but his shouts were not heard in Belpré. He was standing at the horse's head when the gay cavalcade came riding down from Marietta under the green foliage of the woods.

Mrs. Blennerhasset, in flaming habit and plumed hat of white beaver, was in front with her husband, and a negro groom in livery, and the youth of Belpré followed in her train. With her beauty and her high-bred grace and charm she might have appeared so among the canvases of a castle gallery or in the pages of old romance. She knew Johnny at once. Dropping from the saddle, she ran across the beach and gave her hand and the smile that won all hearts.

"What is the trouble?" Her black-lashed blue eyes looked straight into his, and, seeing the pity and perplexity there, she turned and stroked the horse's nose with her gauntleted hand.

Johnny's jaw was set and he swallowed hard. "He has cast his shoes and been overdriven.

The heels are cracked, and the tendons so
sore that— I think he has been beaten
across the legs, and when he dropped he was
left in the woods to starve."

MRS. BLENNERHASSET IN FLAMING HABIT AND PLUMED HAT OF
WHITE BEAVER

She flung her arms around the horse's neck.
"The man who did this should be found and
tied to the whipping-post in Marietta."

"Don't be too hard on him, Margaret. These poor devils of emigrants are in desperate plights sometimes." In his buff small-clothes and silk stockings Mr. Blennerhasset was down in the sand beside the groom. The love of domestic animals and the intelligent care of them were in the blood of this Irish gentleman. He remarked the slender legs and neck and fine coat of the saddle-horse. "Yes," he replied to his wife's appeal, "we'll get him over to the island. Send the poleman back with the ferry. Ransom, go out and help Johnny hold up that horse."

The suffering animal had hobbled back into the water for the grateful coolness about his feet. Johnny and the negro stood at his head on either side and Mr. Blennerhasset fed him with handsful of forage from the woods.

They were there when the *St. Clair* went by, scudding over the white-capped waves. It had a cargo, not only of flour and pork for New Orleans or Havana, but of hopes. The river would never see those homespun sails of flax and hemp again, for the vessel could not be brought back, and months must pass before this doughty Commodore Whipple, who had sunk the *Gaspé* in '72, could return over the mountains with the proceeds of the *St. Clair's* sale in Philadelphia. So every sort of water craft known on Western waters was in its escort down to Louisville, where hearts would stand still until it was safely warped over the falls. Now it was ringed about with the music of Revolutionary fifes and drums, boat bugles, and French violins.

When the pageant had gone by, the silence of the wilderness fell again—a stillness that was woven through and through with water ripple and leaf rustle, then the song of a wood-thrush, wild and sweet.

It was an hour before the horse was got over to the island and into a grassy paddock in the pasture. There he was groomed, and bedded on bright straw, with his feet cleaned and poulticed and his legs bandaged. His bay coat shone in the sun, and he had his head up, giving promise of a beautiful arch to the neck, when Mrs. Blennerhasset appeared at the bars with her brood of sturdy little children. They were all in the rough garb of the country, ready for a tramp.

"You will have a fine, gentle horse, Johnny, when he is cured of his lameness," she said.

7 87

"No, he is yours. A horse like that could not go where I am going."

"What he needs is a tough little Indian pony that can scramble over these murderous hills like a goat and live on underbrush," Mr. Blennerhasset observed. Neither of them knew that Johnny had not a penny in the world, and to him the fact was immaterial.

They all went to the open glade in the forest, where a plot had been prepared for his planting. The place was girdled with enormous trees, draped with woodbines and honeysuckles, and the sunny close, open to the sky, was musical with bird song. Isle le Beau lay in the track of travel of birds and men. The red tribes and the feathered made their seasonal journeys over the river and up and down the western base of the mountains. The trail known as "The Bloody Way," which ran unbroken from Lake Erie to the Gulf, crossed the Ohio at Belpré. Indians were always passing the head of the island, but they seldom stopped, because there was no large game for the hunter. So this green canoe of land, moored in the flood, had become an island of refuge for everything small and defenseless. Mr. Blennerhasset told these things to Johnny as he worked, and added:

"When war comes, your nursery at Belpré may be destroyed, but this is not likely to be molested."

Johnny suddenly stood up. "You think there will be war?"

Mr. Blennerhasset shrugged his shoulders in the old shooting-jacket in which he felt most comfortable. "Nothing is being done to prevent it. When the game is gone and we begin to crowd the Indians there will be trouble. We should be trying to understand their difficulties and to help them. A few of their leaders are educated and far-seeing men. As a boy Logan, the young chief of the Shawnees at Piqua, was a hostage in the home of Captain Logan of Kentucky, and was brought up with the sons of the house. He is living in a good cabin and cultivating a farm —trying to get his own tribe and others to adopt the white man's way of living. When war comes who could estimate the human value of one civilized and prosperous tribe on the border? Logan is working against tremendous odds, and his time is limited. He needs help."

"He shall have it."

Johnny felt himself and his mission swept into the stream of large and tragic events. His host reminded him that white men went into the Indian country at their own risk. Arrangements could be made for him to meet Logan on the river. He came down to Marietta and Belpré every year, at uncertain times, to learn what he could of building, farming and stock-raising.

Johnny shook his head. His own movements would be uncertain, and he could wait on no man. He would seek the Indians in their own territory. Mrs. Blennerhasset suddenly flung out her hands in protest.

"You would perish, and we cannot spare you." Then her proud head, with its coronet of chestnut braids, went up. She had soldier blood in her to meet undaunted the incredible misfortune which waited in her future. Because of their idealism, generosity and trust in their friends, the Blennerhassets were involved to their ruin in the traitorous scheming of Aaron Burr. "But it is worth dying for. This concerns all the Northwest Territory. And remember, Johnny, here is your island of refuge from every mischance of life."

After that it was so still in the sunny glade that the birds, thinking themselves alone, burst into song. Johnny remarked, presently:

"There will be trees here not worth transplanting. We can leave them to make a grove of wild apples for the birds."

"Harman, I sometimes think there are such groves in heaven." The emphasis was on the "are," as if the subject had been discussed before.

Johnny looked up in quick sympathy with the thought, to see Mr. Blennerhasset shake a playful finger at his wife.

"You've been reading that fantastic visionary, Swedenborg, again, Margaret."

She admitted it with a smile of pensive sweetness. They stood there hand in hand, breathing the incense of the wood and listening to Johnny talking to the children about tucking the seeds in soft, warm beds as though they were babies. Dominic, the little son and heir of the house, was cuddling a seed in his brown hand.

"May I keep this one, Johnny?"

"To plant?"

"No. I want to see the little tree in it."

"You can't see it. It's too small."

Johnny had found the germs and watched the wonderful processes of germination in the larger seeds of field and garden, but the apple-seed with its tough case and tiny seed-leaves had baffled him.

"It can be seen under the solar micro-scope," Mr. Blennerhasset assured him. Then, humorously: "Don't be alarmed at the wisdom of my young hopefuls. I've forgotten all I knew at their age, and am having to begin with them where I left off."

It was in the little laboratory, set up in an alcove of a library of *belles-lettres* by this graduate from Dublin University, who had a bent for the natural sciences, that Johnny split the brown shell, parted the seed-leaves on a piercing needle, and fixed the seed under the magic lens. There, hidden away in its inmost heart, was the spark of life breathed in by the Creator—the pearly dot that held the impulse, the longing, to burst its bonds and lift itself up to sun and rain and bird song, and realize itself in blossom, fruit and ripened seed.

To Johnny it was the soul of the apple-tree. He could not talk about it. He had meant to stop at Isle le Beau for the night, but a home-seeker's flatboat tied up at Belpré would be off at sunrise, and on that he hoped he could arrange to work his passage down to the French grant at Galliopolis. So he asked to be set across at once. Mrs. Blennerhasset ran down to the landing with the gift of a pocket compass and a book that he could carry in his food-pouch with his Bible.

"This will interest you, Johnny. It was written by a great natural scientist who came so to know and reverence animal and plant life that he made a new kind of heaven to take in all we love on earth."

It was six weeks before he returned from the West for the portion of the seeds that he had left with Colonel Cushing. Bit by bit, by fire or candle light, or in brief intervals of rest, he had read the burning message of the little book—Swedenborg's *Heaven and Hell*.

It is difficult for us to realize that the brotherhood of man with the lower orders, which is a part of the moral law of to-day, was the new, religious doctrine of a century ago. To people of the gentle feeling and cultivated mind of Mrs. Blennerhasset it had its poetic and humane appeal without disturbing orthodoxy. But to many it was nothing less than a divine revelation, and a few like Johnny accepted it as the only rule of life. Loving all living things as he did, it was easy for him to see, in every flower and bird, creeping worm and aspiring tree, the Indwelling Spirit, and to see them all, in death, translated to the skies in supernal beauty and dwelling with angels in the Garden of God. There it was, the faith that, in every age and clime, and for countless creeds, has fired the souls of men to do impossible and imperishable deeds.

It was a waste of time and energy to combat opposition, so he said nothing of his intentions. Supper had been eaten at the long and laden board, where there was "room for one or two more," when Colonel Cushing began to talk of the earliest years of Belpré.

"One winter we had famine, pestilence and savage war. Shut up in Farmers' Castle we lived on fish without salt; then on maple-sap porridge and boiled nettles. The dogs that lived through it ate green corn when it came in. It's as bad as that to-day, in the back clearings, when a man has a crop failure and gets out of ammunition."

He gave Johnny a hunter's homespun suit, dyed forest green for greater safety in summer, and a package of warrior's bread—parched corn meal and maple sugar—for emergencies, and cautioned him:

"Take plenty of powder and shot, Johnny. There are more wildcats than cabins in these woods, and very little to eat except what runs or flies."

It was late when he went up on the bluff to camp under the cedars, between the river's murmuring flow and the silent stream of stars in the sky, and to take counsel of his soul. In the tender light of a half-moon of pearl the shadows of the bare tree-trunks had the density of black velvet on the dry and odorous bed of needles. Once a keel-boat went by, its long shape slipping through the silver current like a swimming otter. From the next bend below the note of its bugle came back, mellowed by distance and darkness into some ineffable call. Uplifted, Johnny lay in a shining solitude and peace that was like a benediction on his purpose.

The sun was on the water and the dew on

the lawn when he rowed across to Isle le Beau.
The house was as silent as the palace of the
Sleeping Beauty. No one was in the French
drawing-room, nor in the wainscoted hall,
with its fireplace filled with feathery greens,
its gun-rack and antlered heads. In a moment the master and mistress would descend
to the breakfast-room, which was open to
the fresh June morning, and happy children
would come sliding down the only broad
banister in the Northwest Territory. Mrs.
Blennerhasset's garden hat and gloves, rose-
basket and shears, were on the hall table.
Johnny left his gun beside them, and a note
in the basket:

You will understand that I can no longer kill my
little brothers of the earth and air. Thank you for
this news straight from Heaven.

In the cedar grove he changed to the green
suit, and on the edge of the bluff he shouldered
his tools and lightened pack. Looking across
to the island, he saw Mrs. Blennerhasset running down the lawn to the landing, as if she
must overtake him. Waving his hat to the
blowing white draperies at the head of Isle
le Beau, Johnny was gone, defenseless, into
the wilds.

JOHNNY AT PLESSIS

V

ON "THE BLOODY WAY"

T HE region that lay between the lower Muskingum and Scioto, into which Johnny disappeared, was much less wild than that traversed by the Great Trail from Pittsburg to Zanesville. It had been populous even in Indian days, and had its ancient routes of travel. . The trail that ran northeast from Belpré to Big Rock, forty miles above Marietta and opposite the broad meadow of Big Bottom, was an important part of "The Bloody Way," the old warrior's path that ran from Lake Erie to the Gulf. Here red men had leveled the summits of the steepest hills, and piled up embankments where a pony might slip with its rider into eternity. Since the close of the war white settlers had been slowly widening "The Bloody Way" into a wagon-road; and wild animals had long since learned to avoid its ever-fresh odors of gunpowder and passing men. Beside it were safe camping-places that had been used for generations; and the Indians had been careful, in their annual burning of forest undergrowth, not to destroy the fruits and nuts along the trails. Johnny found berries by the wayside to help out the dry meals that he ate on the road.

A dozen creeks that have disappeared today then foamed down the declivities, and their crystal pools swarmed with fish. Along these streams that were crossed by the trail settlers had raised their isolated cabins on the scattered patches of good bottom-land. Johnny often slipped off his moccasins and waded these spring-fed waterways rather than skirt the swamps in the hollows, or struggle through thickets of blossoming laurel on the gravel benches to reach the infrequent house. From any hilltop he could mark the most sinuous course of a creek by the lines of sycamores, and locate a hidden home by the smoke that curled up through the woods.

It was too late in the season to put in seeds

—and too early. He meant to make friends and to select sites for next year's planting; to penetrate the marshy forests and sunny uplands of the Indian country about the head-waters of the Scioto, and to put in what few seeds he had left along the route of his return to the cider-mills in the autumn.

In a land where every man rode because of the unpeopled distances to be covered, and carried a weapon for his safety and a food-supply, it was a startling thing to see that slender youth appear out of the darkening woods, unmounted, undefended, his straw hat filled with wild berries as a welcome addition to the evening meal.

Until his trees were in bearing he must pay his way by other services in that land of bit-ter toil and privation, so, in return for food and shelter, he lent a hand at whatever work was afoot. Besides, he must learn how to do everything that new-comers and Indians needed to know in order to conquer their hard circumstances. He helped raise the cabins of green buckeye logs; he took his turn at plow or scythe or ax, and beat out grain with flails on barn floor or buffalo-hide. He brought in news of every deer-lick he discovered, where men might drive cattle that were perishing for salt. In the useless angles of rail fences he started patches of briers, for with foraging bears about women and children could not go berrying along the trails. He showed the men how to build ash-hoppers, so the women could make lye hominy and soft soap; and one of his self-imposed tasks was the raising of hog-pen walls so high that wolves could not get in.

And, oh, it seemed afterward that what was remembered longest by boys and girls grown tall was that Johnny taught them simple games, invented rude toys, and told them curious and endearing things of the plant and animal life of the forest. This was in the fire-lit evenings when they were little, scared, wood-imprisoned, resourceless children. Schools were not yet possible, and even freedom in play was denied. In the stump-lots about stark cabins they often had not a tree to shade their sunburnt heads or to support a grape-vine swing, and beyond the clearings little ones could not go. There were stories that made faces go gray as ashes, of exploring babies who had gone just beyond corn-fields, and then, where the little foot-

prints stopped in the soft leaf-mold, there
were the tracks of huge cats—

When supper was over and the children in
bed Johnny read aloud to the elders, many of
whom were illiterate. Resting his elbows on
the hearth, he read from the Bible or the other
book. And he told them why and how he
had come into the wilds to plant orchards.
The very words awoke the happiest memories
of many. And what visions of comfort, what
feeling of greater security and companionship, he conjured by his warm, familiar talks!
The trees of the forest that shut them in were
grand, but aloof, living for themselves alone.
But apple-trees were tame and friendly, serv-
ing men and dependent upon their care like
dogs and all gentle domestic animals. As if
yearning for the company of the fireside, an
orchard nestled about a house, extended the
shelter of the roof, made the family feel at
ease out of doors, pushed the wilderness back.
People listening to such talk looked with
something like awe upon his young face of
high courage, religious fervor, and burning
desire to serve them in this practical but
poetic way.

It was a wonderful thing for a pioneer

family, that had all but lost its social instinct and capacity for pleasure, to stop toil for the day and range the summer woods with Johnny, to search out some lovely, guarded nook in which he could hide and defend a nursery. In hearts benumbed the hope was revived that life might be lifted above this lonely and sordid struggle—the burden be lightened by brotherly love such as this.

The country was still very thinly settled, the clearings few and miles apart, but he was directed from one cabin to the next, and seldom lacked food and shelter at night. And when his moccasins were worn out they were replaced by cowhide boots of a farmer's rough cobbling, and his linsey shirt by another of some woman's weaving. Gaunt pioneers wrung his hand at parting and protested at his refusal of a spare gun. Women washed his clothes, refilled his food-pouch, and watched and waved from doorways until he had disappeared. Children followed him to the very edges of clearings, climbed to the tops of rail fences, and cried after him:

"Good-by, Johnny. You'll come back?"

"Oh yes, I'll come back next spring. Good-by, good-by!"

The confident smile made every one believe it until he was gone. But afterward, whenever the howling of wolves or the footfalls of panthers on clapboarded roofs made men rise in the night to replenish fires, women lay wide-eyed in the dark and thought of Johnny.

At Big Rock, opposite Big Bottom, he struck the Muskingum Trail. On this he continued along the west bank of the river up to the Great Crossing. Here there was a junction of trails that shot out across the wooded highlands like the spokes of a wheel. To the north and west were main-traveled roads which led to the valleys of the Cuyahoga and the Scioto; but he turned, instead, into a narrow trace that ran northwestward for one hundred miles to a Shawnee village below Sandusky.

As this was only a hunter's bridle-path the clearings disappeared at once. He was obliged now to camp in some cave-like excavation of a hillside, against the opening of a hollow tree, or under the natural tent of a fox-grape vine, which he strengthened with stakes and his coil of hemp rope. With protection at the back, a fire in front, and a camper's elevated bed of posts, cross-poles and pine boughs to lift himself above creeping reptiles, he was safe enough even from panthers, whose yellow eyes often watched him across the flames. In summer wolves were not driven by hunger and did not hunt in packs, and bears were intent upon keeping out of the way and finding food for their cubs.

Orchards would not be needed in this region for years, so Johnny traveled fast. He found the world a simpler place to live in since it was stripped of anxieties and fears. If he could not kill animals of evil intentions, he could at least avoid them and give them no cause for offense. And in solitude he was no longer lonely. Trees had become to him sentient and beneficent things, drawing their life from the same mother earth that supported himself, and reaching up with love and trust to the same kind sky. So, although birds flitted about in shabby coats, silent and unseen, and animals fed in secret places on nature's abundance, he was companioned on the day march and the night watch by the trees, statuesque and serene.

Every hour brought its thrill of fresh wonder. The climate of Ohio a hundred years ago had no such extremes as it has to-day, or as Johnny experienced before his task was done. Winter frosts and gales, and summer suns, were tempered by the forests, and snow sank deep to bubble up in springs. Even in August there were cooling showers almost daily, and the ground, lush with greenery, was never quite dry except along the wind-swept ridges. And from storm there was shelter. In the columned and canopied woods rain reached the turf only by running down mossy trunks, or after being shattered to spray on the leaf-thatching above. It was sweet to tread the valleys in the green gloom and noon-day hush of the year—to splash across tumbling brooks, to scramble up oozy banks, to mount the slopes of giant hardwoods to the music of chuckling springs, and to come up, at last, into a grove of oaks and pines and look out over an emerald sea of trees.

Long before he reached the Indian country his last bit of dry food was gone. Bears were in every blackberry thicket and declined to share their feast. Some days he found nothing to eat besides half-ripe plums, and wild oats in patches that were full of the soft whistling of quail. He had difficulty in locating safe camping-places and, foot-sore and half famished, made slow progress up and down the interminable hills.

One night he found shelter in a salt-maker's camp, where a brine well had been sunk through an old deer-lick. The iron kettles, bubbling under a rude shed, the smoke and steam and noxious odors, and the unkempt workers who slept by shifts in a cave and lived almost wholly by the chase, made a mythical labor of punishment. But with salt eight dollars a bushel and all but unobtainable, no work of the backwoods was more necessary or truly heroic, and Johnny was glad to hear that a better field had been found down on the Scioto. There these men could have their families, build up a farm village, and live like human beings. He made a note of the new location to which they intended to move in the spring, and promised to put in a nursery there. But from a place that reeked with slaughter he departed hungry.

As he neared the top of the watershed the undulations of the land became broader and shallower. But traveling was not easier, for large rivers had their head-waters in the lakes and streams that spread and wandered over wide, marshy valleys.

It was near sunset one day when he saw in such a wet, wooded depression a cabin that had seemingly been abandoned before it was finished. A skin curtain flapped in the opening, but there was no smoke from the stick-and-clay chimney which stopped short of the ridge-pole in a hole that a wolf could leap through. But corn had been planted, and here was food if bears had not stripped the stalks of ears. So near starvation that he staggered as he ran, Johnny splashed up the creek-bed and skirted the swamp below the clearing.

A woman whose hair blew loose about a distracted face was crouched with a frightened child in the darkest corner of a hovel that was a trap rather than a shelter. She had screamed and fled when she heard the running man, but when she saw Johnny's face she sobbed out excuses in the dear, broken German that had welcomed him at many a comfortable fireside in Pennsylvania:

"All voods! It vas schust so vild here I go crazy."

She sat there talking in a dreary monotone.

The husband was a blacksmith and had no farm or building tools, and others who had bought land here had not come. The house furnishings had been lost by an upset in a stream. The cow had wandered away. The baby had died. There was a little grave—heaped above her heart. Her husband had gone to trade the horse for meal and powder. Then the fire had gone out in the night and she could not build another. There had been nothing to eat all day, but that would not matter if she could just see smoke by somebody's house. So lonely! So homesick!

"We'll have some smoke from our house, and that will be more friendly," Johnny said, reassuringly. He had seen people in desperate situations, but no such wretchedness as this. Here was a soul defeated and flickering into darkness.

He whistled a martial old hymn tune that should have put backbone into an angleworm as he whittled shavings from a pine branch. Then he poured a spoonful of the powder, that he carried for quick fire-building, on the hearth and struck a spark from flint and steel. With a little explosion cheerful flames leaped up the chimney. The corn was neither ripe nor in the milk, but Johnny set the woman to scoring the hardening grains and pressing out the pulp. Cakes salted from the black and bitter lump given him at the camp were wrapped in husks and put to bake in hot ashes. And then the hovel was furnished forth with the laughter of a child and with a good woman's tears—natural tears, now— that she had nothing better to give this heaven-sent guest to eat.

It was in the evening of the next day that the husband and father literally fell into the cabin under the weight of a hundred pounds of meal that he had carried forty miles. But he had good news. Two families were coming—farmers. There would be neighbors, and work that he could do. Before he slept he began with frantic haste to set up the rusting fittings of a smithy.

Johnny did not leave this place until the new-comers were in their half-faced camps, axes were ringing in the timber, and hinges and cranes were being beaten out of old horse-shoes and wagon tires on the anvil. A crop of turnips could still be grown, nuts gathered, a bee-tree felled, and forage cut in woodland glades. He cleared and fenced a well-drained and sheltered slope for the nursery that he promised to plant six weeks later. It was thus that he helped, in the beginning, at many a clearing or forlorn little settlement that sprang up and lived precariously all along the border for the next dozen years, and then bore the first shock of savage war.

He had not walked a mile along the trace before he was aware of a violet haze as of Indian summer. The tribes, he knew, did not burn the forest undergrowth until the windless days that came after a sharp frost. It was then that they journeyed with the creeping fires, which they herded carefully, to the hunting-grounds in the East. Some settler in the next valley must be burning brush. He turned back at once to warn the good people he had just left not to set the woods on fire when burning their brush, and not to kill the bears and deer as long as they were running with their young. Those practices were destructive of game and serious offenses to the Indians. They must keep the peace with their red neighbors.

For two hours he walked in growing apprehension, for the western sky was darkening with a bank of drifting smoke. This mingled with storm-clouds which boiled up in the southwest and spread a pall over the forest. As he topped a rise the slope of burning trees lay below him, beyond a wide, marshy creek. A man watched it from the door of a cabin. The fire had been working slowly down the side of the clearing, in small swamp timber, but now it flared up, turned and raced with the wind.

Johnny ran down into the water, and, heedless of what venomous things might lurk there, struggled across the bog, tripping in wire-like tangles of wild pea-vines and morning-glories. He shouted to the man to shoot his gun or blow a horn. The Shawnee village must be near enough for the Indians to hear an alarm. They would run to help put that fire out before it gained headway.

"You mind your own business! I started that fire—easier than chopping down trees!" When Johnny stopped, too shocked to speak, he shouted, angrily: "What's the matter with you? Them trees are mine, ain't they?"

"They're God's trees! Look! You've loosed a devil of destruction that no one can stop!"

The fellow did turn pale, for the wind had

whipped around and risen to a gale that swept the flames up the hillside in a moaning sigh. Forest giants shriveled before they were engulfed by that billow of fire. On the crest a pine-tree flashed into a torch.

Then flying creatures made for water—deer bounding away; a singed wolf running and howling like a tortured dog; a bear shambling out and woof-woofing for her cubs. Johnny ran up through the corn into the burning wood and headed the clumsy, near-grown babies toward their mother. Hearing cries of agony, smelling scorching fur, seeing a flight of wood-pigeons drop like shot into that furnace, Johnny stumbled out and threw his arm up to protect his eyes from flying sparks. Amid all that horror he heard the crack of a rifle. The she-bear lay dead on the marsh, and the cubs turned back into the blazing forest. The man dodged into the cabin.

On the farther bank of the creek a young Indian brave who had an eagle feather in his beaded head-band, but who wore the green shirt and buckskin breeches of the white hunter, stood with his rifle aimed at the cabin door. As Johnny ran toward him, calling out,

**JOHNNY SAGGED FORWARD ON THE PONY UPON WHICH
THE INDIAN SET HIM**

in what little Shawnese he knew, not to do murder and start a border war, there were two reports almost together. Then the door clattered shut.

It was the Indian who saw the blood that streamed down Johnny's hand. In surly silence he cut away the soaked sleeve and knotted it above the wound in the arm. Then he rushed him up under a beech-tree, the safest woodland shelter in the thunder-storm which suddenly fell upon them.

In a half-hour the summer tempest was over. The sun sank through banks of splendor, behind the ruin on the hillside. Johnny sagged forward on the pony upon which the Indian set him with his pack and tools, as he rode past the tract of blasted trees. And he stood in the Shawnee village, when the story was told, involved in this fresh crime of one of his own race against the law of the forest. This was a different band from the one he had met in friendly ways in the East, the faces all strange. Besides hatred and suspicion they showed a frank contempt for this ragged white stripling in whose thin face the dark eyes shone unnaturally large and bright.

The brave who had brought him in appeared to be a distinguished visitor from another tribe. He spoke to Johnny briefly and in as good English as his own. Because he had had no hand in that fire they would dress his wound and set him in safety across the border in the morning. Seeing that he had neither horse nor gun, he could not have far to go.

"That bullet was meant for me. It must be cut out."

Johnny extended his arm at once, and stood as steady as a rock while a knife explored the furrow and turned out the ball. The Indian put the bullet in his pocket for a future use that was unmistakable. He watched Johnny curiously while the wound was being washed and the ragged edges trimmed.

"A brave would burn it, and then cure the burn."

Johnny himself laid on the searing-iron. To the red man the stoic endurance of torture is the supreme test. When the wound had been spread with a healing ointment and bandaged, the Indian led Johnny to his own guest-lodge and bade a squaw fetch him a bowl of corn soup.

Then at once he seemed to forget that

Johnny was there. A noble figure of a man, he stood in deep abstraction, with his head bent and his fists clenched at his sides. Afterward Johnny learned that he was of a historic line of warriors—a nephew of Tecumseh and The Prophet—but one who led his people into the paths of industry and peace. After a time he took the blood-stained bullet from his pocket, looked at it reflectively as if weighing many things, and then stooped deliberately and pushed it into the earth. As if relieved of that burden of revenge, the whole man relaxed, and he turned a grave and not unfriendly look on Johnny.

"You were right. He is an evil man. But it would profit us nothing to kill him. We must learn to live like white men. But give us time—give us time!" His voice shook with passion. "When I see a white savage like that destroying the food and shelter of my poor people I am all Indian."

"Logan!" Johnny whispered. "Is it Chief Logan?"

After a wonderful hour he lay alone on his bed of soft skins. The flap of the lodge was tied back. He could see the circle of braves squatted about the council fire, and hear

Logan's plea for his mission of love, which was meant to help lift the red tribes above the tragic chances of the chase. At midnight the young chief lay down beside him, threw his arm across, and in the darkness and silence spoke the eloquent word:
"Brother!"

Johnny's arm was still useless, and Logan had gone back to Piqua with a buckskin pouch of apple-seeds and minute instructions concerning them, when he put in the first of the few nurseries that he was encouraged to plant in the Indian country. It was in a little hollow of the hills which was full of the burning bushes of sumach and the flickering fires of sassafras. Squaws cleared and broke up the ground and wove the stout barrier across the open side, and papooses carried his tools and seeds, and fetched kettles of water. They all promised to watch in the spring for the rows of bright-barked twigs, and to keep the soil loose and free from weeds until his return.

He journeyed eastward with the hunters. From every height the autumn landscape rolled away in colors of sunset. On sharp mornings there were hoar frosts as thick and sparkling as snow, and into every sylvan camp the light was sifted through a vast, jeweled lantern. Leaves drifted down, nuts pattered, squirrels scrambled to get in their winter stores, birds took their last feast of seeds, flocks of bronze turkeys fattened in the amber chestnut groves. The creeping fires in the forest undergrowth mingled their smoke with the still air of Indian summer, making a pungent atmosphere as silvery a blue as the fringed gentians. It brooded over the primeval world like a tender memory of all the years that had died in just such splendid tranquillity and the faith of spring.

Spring was hurrying up the foot-hill valleys of the western slope again when Johnny re-appeared in a camp on the Great Trail. Although their ponies were loaded with furs, jerked venison and bears' grease, the Indians managed to get his apple-seeds to the Great Crossing. There he lashed two borrowed canoes together and floated down the Muskingum, stopping to put his nurseries in order and to replant those that had not survived.

Leaving half his seeds at Isle le Beau, he went by the route of the summer before up to the Shawnee village. But he traveled faster now, on relays of horses furnished by white settlers, and then on a pony, for a band of Indians came far down the trace to meet him. Along the Scioto he put in a nursery at the new salt-maker's camp, and wherever there was the floating mill and blacksmith shop that made the nucleus of a settlement. Over the old Scioto-Beaver trail he crossed to the Muskingum.

It was June when he returned to Marietta, to find Kitt Putnam hoeing and weeding in the flowery cove above the shipyard, and to find rows and rows of apple-twigs, bright-barked as rose - canes, tall enough for boys' switches and showing sturdy bunches of fuzzy, gray-green foliage.

9

VI

A VISION OF ROMANCE

WHEN Betty Stacey married at seventeen, and went away back in the woods to live on a little creek that ran singing to the Scioto, Johnny planted his first orchard near the Indian border about the new home.

The year before he had arrived at Marietta early in March, when the red maples were dropping their crimson blossoms on the last patches of snow. Along the Muskingum he had found some of his nurseries overrun by deer or choked by weeds. In none of them, indeed, except at Zanesville and Big Bottom, were there more than a few trees worth transplanting. But those few, set out by cabin doors, and Johnny's undaunted spirit, stimulated hope and stiffened determination in the sparsely settled districts. He cleared the plantations again, strengthened the broken barriers, replanted the plots, and gave them to the care of the best men to be found. And he told people not to be discouraged. This was just a beginning, and he was young and life long. Better luck next time.

But here in Marietta, with a town full of vigilant people on guard, and Dr. True in authority over Kitt Putnam, everything had prospered. The happy day of toil that he spent in the hollow above the shipyard began with a rush of wings. From long journeys little bundles of feathers and bursts of song fell from the sky. On the morrow he meant to have here a gathering of the heads of households for the first distribution of trees, and for instruction in the setting out and care of them.

First he thinned the rows, with a swift certainty of eye and hand discarding all plants of feeble growth. A few tough little twisted witches, that could be trusted to put out defensive thorns and hold their own in the wilds he planted among the hawthorns, dogwood and Judas-trees in the edges of the forest, for their beauty of blossom. Then he carefully lifted the trees that had shot up almost to his own height, with stout, straight trunks, bright bark, healthy buds and low, symmetrical branching. These he pruned back, trimmed the roots neatly, and banked in a trench all ready for transplanting. Stock of good trunk and root growth, but with unpromising tops, he cut off to a point near the ground and replanted in one row for grafting with buds from Dr. True's Summer Sweeting. He meant to rob that noble tree of more buds, wrap them in wet moss and carry them down to Belpré and Isle le Beau, even to Galliopolis, if possible, where bewildered exiles mourned the lost orchards and gardens of their dear France.

It was late in the afternoon before the plantation was denuded. He had begun to prepare the ground for new seeds when a little boy appeared from the shipyard, where four vessels lay on the ways and there was much thrilling adventure to be had scrambling over the rigging. To any child it was fascinating play to help Johnny in his work, and he was never too busy to listen to shy confidences or to answer endless questions. This boy asked if it was true, as Dominic

Blennerhasset said, that the littlest thread-roots of trees were hollow and had mouths for drinking water.

Johnny did not know, but he thought it very likely. Sugar maples must drink like river pike. Children with sharp ears could hear the sap run up. He would look through the microscope at Isle le Beau, and find out about that. And here his thought was off on the wings of wonder and joy, that the world was so ordered in use and beauty that rain from the sky was miraculously turned to winey juice in the glowing chalices of apples.

The child had been in the cove an hour before he began to tell the news of the town: "Dr. True stays at Aunt Mary Lake's nearly all the time, and Betty comes to our house when she wants to cry."

Johnny dropped his hoe and stared. "Why does the doctor— Why does Betty want to cry?"

"I guess it's because Aunt Mary's been awful sick a long time. She don't get out of bed at all."

Mary Lake dying! No, nothing died! For Johnny not a flower drooped on its stalk, nor a sparrow fell, whose perfume and song had not their lovelier counterparts on the other shore. But Mary Lake fading from the eyes that dwelt on her, the hearts that loved her, on earth! And this was not a time of death, but of resurrection. Countless pale but pulsing things were coming up out of winter tombs. The bluebird trilled to his mate; and Johnny had been conscious of strange stirrings in himself, an eagerness of foot and eye, a bubbling up of all the springs of youth.

In the garrison inclosure of Campus Martius it was so very still—only a group of silent women drawing water for the evening meal at the well, and children hushed at play— that he could hear the purple martins taking their last wheeling flights in the dusk. Dr. True sat outside the door, his hickory chair tilted against the wall, every line of his lank figure confessing sadness and defeat.

"I'd have had Mary Lake well in no time, Johnny, if she had been up to help me," he said, his humor whimsical even in his grief.

A neighbor woman was bending over the bed. She had had to fetch her young baby, and Betty was sitting with it in Johnny's low rocking-chair, her bright hair burnished by the firelight. At sixteen she had grown tall and fair, and was now so tenderly maternal as she looked down upon the little bit of a darling thing in her arms. Johnny had come in so softly that she did not hear him, and his heart seemed to stop beating as memories of old dreams crowded back upon him. It was as if he had just come in from the orchard at Pittsburg, and the breeze from the opening door had set the little chair, with its haunting vision of all that was meant by love and home, in motion. The strangest thing about it was that he knew— When Betty lifted her eyes to his he saw the sweet, sweet face for which he had looked under the hoods of a thousand caravans.

He gripped the door-post and had himself in hand by the time she had laid the baby down and run to him. She stretched out her hands in glad welcome, but her lips were tremulous with trouble and her blue eyes were suddenly flooded.

"It's not for Aunt Mary, Johnny," she said. "She has no pain, now, and is so happy. It's just that, when she's gone, there will be no one in the world belonging to me."

Unconscious of the nature or the power of that appeal to him, she went away presently with the neighbor, and remained to cry her heart out where it would not distress Aunt Mary, while Johnny watched by the bed.

That wood-nest of a low-ceiled, quiet room seemed thronged with grateful spirits. How many lives had been ushered in there! How often had death been turned from that door! Johnny waited until Mary Lake stirred at the note of a distant bugle, a sound that he never could hear without a thrill. Her dim eyes rested upon him with the vision of those who look back from the parting veil. Did she foresee the long journey of life that lay before him, and have the tender wish that it might not be uncompanioned?

"Dear lad—you would be—the core of the heart—of the woman—who loved you."

He thought only of Betty. "Aunt Mary," he asked, gently, not to call her too far back, "what is to become of Betty?"

There was the faintest, untroubled smile. "Do 'ee think—the pretty maid—will not marry?"

His voice choked on the answer: "Yes, she

will marry—early. But does—does she love any one now?"

It was moments before Mary Lake replied. She gazed at Johnny wistfully, and then around the dear, familiar room, as if she would see another family of her own heart's choosing sheltered there. "A young maid—does not love any one—enough—until she is asked. Do 'ee—"

At that moment Betty returned. A tiny girl in a linsey slip followed her and stood expectantly within the doorway. The shy little figure could have been no more than a shadow to those failing eyes, and the lisping "pleathe" could not have reached her ears, but Mary Lake knew. She was dying, but so busy doing things for the least of these little ones that she just forgot about it.

"Do 'ee—give her—a cooky—my dear."

The child was gone, sucking the sweet as blissfully, as unthinking of the source of that bounty, as a butterfly on a flower. Then on the closed room there fell such a silence that the swallows could be heard settling in their nests about the eaves. Johnny still knelt, and Betty was in a desolate heap at his feet, the cooky-jar tilted on her lap and spilling its treasure on the floor. The overflow was a part of the loving - kindness that now streamed down from the sky.

No one had gone out of the house, but in a moment it was as if a messenger had been abroad. The doctor was in the room, neighbors, and weeping young girls who had the dear privilege of putting their arms around and comforting Betty. But in an hour the face of death was covered and the routine of life taken up again. Some one mended the fire and hung the kettle. The doctor was called away, and one by one the women departed to attend to their own household duties. With that hourly responsibility for the physical needs of others which left pioneer women little time for grief, Betty laid the table and turned on Johnny a look of affectionate concern.

"You've had a long day's work. Won't you try to eat a little supper? Please, Johnny."

He patted her hand gently, and, sitting down with her in the intimacy of sorrow ate a bowl of mush and milk. But it was almost more than he could bear. When others came in to watch, and Betty slept, still sobbing in her sleep, Johnny went out into a night that glittered with frosty stars. Between the tall shafts of leafless trees he went up Sacra Via to the Big Mound, and lay among the scattered headboards of God's Acre, alone with his temptation.

From a heart that had long lain dormant love had quickened in the fires of spring to vivid and insistent life. Without seeking, and to his profound dismay, he had found her, and alone, bereft, unprotected. He must stay with her, win her, defend her in these perilous wilds that lay under the gathering clouds of war, wear her on his breast. He knew that he could protect her better than most men in that region. How would it be with him if he left her and she perished?

Even his work had shaped itself as if to this end of personal happiness. Only near the few large settlements did it seem probable that his nurseries could flourish, or any great number of people be served. To a dozen such places along the river westward to Vincennes he could make semi-annual journeys by the mail - packet and freight-pirogues. Enough money could be got for his trees to employ help to care for them and to pay men to wash out seeds at the cider-mills. Here in Marietta he could have the farm that had been offered him by the Ohio Company, build up such another home as he had had in Pittsburg, and provide for a family within the safe shelter of the guns of Fort Harmer. And by and by, when the wilder beasts were gone, and the Indians had become civilized or,—when the Indians, too, were gone, so that Betty would not be afraid, they could have a green little home in a bowering orchard in the forest.

He need only give up that part of his mission which took him into the backwoods— say that the task could not be done, and men would believe him. But he knew that he had been taking something more than the promise of orchards into the wilds — himself, brotherly love, unselfish service, the hope of better days. And in a dozen years, a tree like Dr. True's here and there would begin to leaven the bare clearings. He would know that the task was not impossible, and that knowledge would poison all his relations with men, with wife and child and God. And the nurseries he had planted and abandoned would blush for him in thorny thickets every

spring, a reminder of one man's broken promise undermining the faith of men.

He had made his covenant. The work to
which he had consecrated himself would fill
the measure of his years to the brim, and need
all the passion that burned within him.

After the funeral and the distribution of
trees Johnny went down to Belpré and Isle
le Beau in the Blennerhassets' big canoe with
six negro rowers, leaving Betty to make a
home temporarily for Dr. True, heart-free and
for another man's wooing. And this was the
spring of the year and the mating season in
his soul, when the courtship-caroling of bluebird, wood-thrush, and oriole pierced the
heart of youth with their sweetness.

That summer he went up through Cincinnati and Dayton to Piqua. There for a
month he lay ill from a snake - bite, and
was cared for in the good log house of Chief
Logan. It was a heartening thing to find,
on the bank of the Miami, even this one small
band bravely struggling to learn the difficult
habits and arts of a rude civilization. A number of cabins, barns and corn-cribs had been
built; fields were being tilled with wooden

mold-board plows, and cattle tended in fenced pastures. Squaws heckled flax and worked at wheel and loom. In the autumn the trees of a flourishing nursery could be set out. Before he left the village Johnny planted a little apple-tree for the braves, and gave them brief instructions as to the proper care of an orchard to bring it to its greatest use and beauty.

When able to travel he was given a pony for the season, provided with food, and set upon the cross-country trail that ran from the Miami to the Scioto. It was on the moraine where the hills had been rounded and the valleys filled with fine drift by the ancient ice-cap. There were few boulders, but every crystal-clear stream rippled over a bed of pebbles, and enormous hardwood trees were rooted deep in clean, gravelly loam.

One evening late in August, as he topped a steep rise after fording a creek, he looked down into such a sylvan retreat as he had imagined for that green little home in the forest with Betty. Noble trees, set far apart and with little undergrowth, stepped down the turfed terraces of a natural amphitheater to an open glade where deer had long been

accustomed to graze. Across the front of this
the creek had turned and widened in peaceful flow toward the Scioto. Willows fringed
the banks, and from the grassy slopes wood-
lilies lifted their chalices of flame and painted
moccasin-flowers danced on every breeze.

He stopped for no more than a moment to
look down from the trail, and was riding on
when he saw, at one side of the glade, a
smoldering log in front of a new-comer's half-
faced camp. Then he heard a hallooing from
the woods, and was dragged from the pony
by young David Varnum of Marietta.

"Whoopee, Johnny! If this isn't luck!
I'm so almighty glad to see you I could sa-
lute you like those fool *parley vous* at Galliopolis."

Johnny smiled. "If you did I would turn
the other cheek, David. My name is Jonathan." There was healing for sick fancy in
this warm comradeship with one of his own
age and of the New England breed.

"Well, I'll admit it. I'm as pleased as
pie. Been a hermit of the woods here for a
month, and losing my wits and pride for
lonesomeness."

To find him here alone, grubbing out brush,

felling trees, and girdling the buckeye-trees that were used for cabin-building, could mean but one thing. It was thus that an educated and God-fearing Puritan youth carved out a place to stand on in the backwoods of the Northwest Territory, brought his Bible and his wife, defended his own, served his country in camp and court, and by and by built school-houses, churches, roads and bridges. Such men peopled and conquered every American frontier, were loved by their families, honored by their neighbors, and held fast their broad acres for their children's rich inheritance. But from Plymouth Rock to the Golden Gate very few of them ever took the hand of a red man in friendship, spared a harmless animal, or a tree for its age and beauty, or stopped to listen to the song of a meadow-lark.

While stirring a pot of mush over the fire Johnny speculated on David's choice, hoping it might be some maid of Spartan courage who was coming to such a sparsely settled region so far up near the border. Then the soft whistling died on his lips as he remembered David's tender concern for Betty at Mary Lake's funeral. He did not wait.

When David came up from the creek with a fish Johnny laid on the searing-iron that was to cure the wound in his heart.

"Is it Betty Stacey, David?"

"It's Betty. The Lord has been mighty good to me."

Johnny held out his hand in yearning friendship to Betty's lover. "When?"

"Next spring. It will take me all winter here to get ready for her."

"She—she must love you a great deal. You know about her mother? Betty is afraid of the Indians."

David's smile was grim. "I'll take particularly good care that the Indians are afraid of me."

"Oh, make friends with them. It would be safer and happier for Betty."

David shrugged his broad shoulders. "You can't make friends with wildcats and rattlesnakes." Something in Johnny's troubled look made him add: "Why, bless your good heart, Johnny, I'll take care of Betty!"

His self-confidence was pathetic. His uncompromising and contemptuous attitude toward the ten thousand warriors whom he would have as neighbors could not but increase the peril of everything that belonged to him. Johnny remembered the pallid face and wide eyes that Betty had turned on him in the cove, and her apprehension on the bluff below Campus Martius. Then he had reassured her: "The Indians are friendly with me. I'll look after those babies, Betty." David must listen to him, must let him help take care of Betty.

After an unhappy night which was disturbed by wild alarms, he woke to an August morning that was one vast bubble of blue and gold. At the bottom of that dazzling immensity lay this dewy glade, bordered by brown water and guarded by such kind brothers of great trees as must shade the banks of the River of Life.

And here was this conqueror of the wilderness, in the flush of his youthful strength and successful love, talking eagerly of his plans. He meant to put the cabin here, in this natural opening, and then clear the land about it up to the curving trail.

As if he had not heard, Johnny continued to gaze out across the creek and over miles of softly rolling wooded hills and flashes of bright water.

"Your home will be as beautiful as Isle le Beau."

David smiled. "It takes money to live like that. The house is a mansion, as fine as any on the Potomac."

"But they have left the out-of-doors much as God made it. Every pioneer, just by leaving some things alone, could have his own little island of beauty, comfort and safety for his family and domestic animals."

Johnny's look had rested on David wistfully, but now his gray eyes darkened and blazed with indignation.

"The Lord has been good to you in giving you Betty Stacey, but how will you be good to her? I wonder that you dare bring her here at all. And you would turn her beautiful home into a scar on creation, and shut her in, a life prisoner in a hideous, snake-fenced corn-patch? She'll come to you singing like a thrush, and in a year she'll scream if a shadow falls across the door or a tree cracks in the frost."

"Like those— I've seen such women in the back clearings—thought they were bad-tempered or half crazy."

Johnny shook his head. "Just scared to

death, starved for beauty and company, broken-hearted. Men have errands—trust them for dropping work for a day and seeking the society of other men. You have been here alone for only a month, and 'losing your wits and pride for lonesomeness.' But women must stay at home. Their task is never done; little clinging fingers never loose their hold. They are left, wherever and whenever it pleases men to leave them—world without end."

"I might have done that to Betty!" David listened in eagerness and humility to Johnny's plan to fence in this depression, except along the water-front, with puncheon pickets close-set and ten feet high, leaving the crest of the ridge and the trees on the sky-line. When that fence was screened with forest vines and shrubs there would be a little green and flower-walled world of several acres of lawn and garden, bowering orchard and pleasant pasture; and to the sunny south one lovely and limitless view.

David threw up his hands in mock despair. "This is the best grain land of the whole section."

"Then it's none too good for a home. If

A VISION OF ROMANCE

Adam had been an American pioneer he'd have asked for an ax and a gun to improve on Eden. And make it your first business to get some neighbors, so Betty can 'see smoke by somebody's house.'" And Johnny told that story.

Before noon he was gone to the tender nurseries that called to him all along the border, the upper reaches of the Scioto, and the lake shore from the Wyandot village at Sandusky to the struggling settlement at Cleveland. His was but the pause of a bird of passage in that wildwood glade, but because of its timeliness Betty found her island of refuge on the border.

After a rapid journey down the Muskingum and Ohio in the next spring, to distribute trees and put in new seed, Johnny went up to David's clearing. The cabin of logs was up, and the fence—a labor of Hercules, for every tall picket had been split by hand out of black walnut, and secured by hickory pegs driven in auger-holes. The chimney was a great bay of field stones on the gable end, and a low, rock spring-house dairy was snuggled under a sycamore above a pool on the creek bank. A clearing had been made and furrows turned for corn, wheat and flax down the waterway, and the bridegroom had gone away to Marietta.

Johnny had brought up young apple-trees in a canoe from his nursery at Chillicothe, and Betty was to fetch roots and shrubs, bulbs and seeds from the wonderful gardens at Isle le Beau. From rough hillsides and rich woodland nooks he transplanted hawthorn, dogwood, redbud, laurel, elderberry, hazel, wildroses and brier-berries around the fence. Before the puncheon door he set up a tiny stoop of sassafras saplings, and planted wild honeysuckle to clamber over it. Up the gables of the log barn he trained fox-grapes and trumpet-vines. Then down the sloping lawn he made a gravel path to the springhouse, and opened bordering beds for flowering annuals.

Here and there he put in his apple-trees, without any regularity but with a view to effect that would have appeared to a landscape gardener. Not for a generation or more would there be a market for apples in this region, but a settler of the unusual resources and qualities of leadership of David Varnum must make generous provision for less fortunate neighbors, for Indians whose friendship was to be won by hospitality, and for the wayfarers whose numbers would increase with the seasons. And in a region where land was cheap and life dear, it mattered not at all whether a tree paid for the room it occupied. Many of Johnny's trees were planted and cherished for their beauty.

A butternut-tree shaded the well. Across from it he put in a one-sided apple-tree that would unfurl a banner of bloom over the penthouse of white oak. Two trees he set near together to make a tent of boughs above a rustic seat. Separating the kitchen garden from the lawn was one straight row to shelter a colony of beehives. A tree with bent twigs that promised a low, roomy crotch he placed in full view of the front door, where the littlest baby could climb into it under the mother's watchful eye.

In that porous forest soil apple-trees needed no fertilizer and but little cultivation. To plant a tree Johnny dug a big hole and spread the trimmed roots in it. Then he sifted in the moist earth, and pressed it down into a firm bed without using any water. Frequent showers could be depended upon. He tucked the grass and clover sod snugly about the trunk to protect the roots, removed every sucker, pruned the branches back to lower and spread the head, and presently this tame foster-child of the wilderness was putting out new branches and fuzzy bunches of foliage.

Johnny was aware that news of what he was doing would soon be abroad. The place lay on the trail to Piqua, and near a great junction of those "threads of the soil" that met at the terminal of the Scioto - Beaver trail from the east. And he kept a plume of smoke curling up by day and flames glowing by night so that many travelers, white and red, found him out. He meant Betty's home to be the little leaven that should leaven the solitude, hostility and privation of the wilds, a place of physical, social and spiritual refreshment.

He would not have had the house better than it was. The poorest pioneer could have such a shelter. The door was hung on leather hinges; the hearth would be swept with a corn-husk broom. The puncheon floor was so rough that the task of keeping it scoured might well prove discouraging, so Johnny smoothed that as best he might with hatchet

and draw-knife. Then he laid the fire—
back-log, front-log, dry sticks, pine knots,
splinters—ready for lighting with flint and
steel and bit of tow-string. The empty shell
of a place was as rustic as one of the bark
nests he had cunningly set like a knot-hole
in the butternut-tree for bluebirds to move
into. But Betty was one of those gifted
women who could make a cozy home in a
cave.

All the birds were nesting, and night after
sleepless April night Johnny followed that
migrating human pair in tortured fancy from
the gay and tender wedding in Marietta.
They would come to Chillicothe by freight-
pirogue. There David had left his horses
and bought a cow, and there he would hire
a covered wagon for the journey up the river
trail.

That wedding journey through this un-
spoiled wilderness! By night they would
camp in the caravan, for Betty would be
afraid of prowling beasts. She would snuggle
closer to her brave man if but a little owl
hooted. Always alone, watched over by
moon and stars, canopied by new-leafing trees,
waking to all the sweet, stirring life of the

woods and to the wonder of having each
other, moving on in shade and shine and
shower, they would come by slow, blissful
stages to the new life in the new home.

One evening he heard the tramp of horses,
the jolting of the clumsy caravan, and the
lowing of the weary, homesick cow on the
trail. He ran up the grassy terraces and set
the wagon-gate ajar; then ran down to light
the fire on the hearth. But when David
pulled the horses up before the door Johnny
was gone.

Night was falling, and David and Betty
hurried to get Mary Lake's good furniture
in place. Soon the four-poster bed was up
and spread with the hand-woven, blue-and-
white coverlid. Flax-wheel and loom were
set against the wall, and on the cherry dresser
was displayed the scant array of pewter and
blue Canton ware, with the cooky-jar of brown
crockery in the place of honor. An oak
settle filled one chimney-corner, and the little
rocking-chair stood in the other. Black bear
skins warmed the floor. The kettle was bubbling merrily when Betty came to the door
to call Johnny to supper.

She had disappeared in a linsey-curtained

corner for a few moments, and there had been gay, teasing laughter in the single big room that was all in a splendid glow of firelight. Then in the May-queen gown and veil that Mrs. Blennerhasset had given her she stood in the doorway, peering into the odorous dusk.

"He can't be far away. I thought he'd like to see me in my wedding finery. It's so sweet here, David; so dear and safe and happy. The night is full of flowers and stars and dew and sleepy little birds. Where are you, Johnny? Won't you come in? Please, Johnny!"

She went into the cabin at last, disappointed and thoughtful, and put on a girlish frock of blue linsey. Supper was eaten and cleared away. By and by David shut the door. When the fire was covered there was but the faintest glow at the small, oiled-paper windows. The latch-string was pulled in. A whippoorwill cried in the willows.

VII

THE HOME ON THE INDIAN BORDER

I N no year of his mission did Johnny set his feet on the road to the west with such a feeling of well-being and happiness as in the spring of 1811. A general thaw that broke the back of winter in the middle of February brought him into Pittsburg with his seeds. By starting ten days sooner than usual he could get through with the work he had mapped out for the early part of the season, and reach Betty's home for a day's rest in apple-blossom time. At least once in every year it was necessary to reassure himself that Betty and her babies were safe and happy in their little Eden on the border.

In the other book which had become a second Bible to him, there was a text that explained how zeal had lent wings to his purpose:

146

"He arrives sooner who eagerly desires it."
Beyond all he had dared hope, his labor of
love had prospered. As population increased
his nurseries everywhere were cared for; and
once his trees were planted fewer of them died
or reverted to their wild ancestry than had
been the experience in the east. They came
into full bearing much earlier, and, unless restrained by pruning, shot up as tall as forest
trees. Even in the wildest backwoods clearings, where scant attention could be given
them by hard-pressed pioneers, they bore
small but abundant fruit of a mellowness and
spicy flavor such as no ungrafted tree would
bear in the worn-out soils of to-day.

Late in his third winter among the cider-
mills Dr. True, who was obliged to go up to
Pittsburg for medical supplies, went through
a number of old orchards with him. On the
quick return trip by the mail-packet he had
taken buds wrapped in wet moss and hemp
bagging, and grafted them on the young
nursery stock in the cove. Year after year
there had been persistent and intelligent co-
operation with Johnny, and Marietta and
Belpré would soon have all the old favorite
varieties of apples in their orchards, and there

would be fruit to ship to New Orleans. Grafts from the first of these good trees were now being carried westward and up the larger tributaries.

His nurseries must be kept up to supply the ever-increasing flood of new-comers with trees; but Johnny had trained caretakers for his plantations now, and, given seeds, much of his work could be left to them. This released him to press his mission more vigorously in the Indian country. Conditions had long been working ruin for the tribes of the Northwest, and their growing poverty and helplessness was a piteous thing.

In the winter Indians still hunted in the eastern hills, but with diminishing returns for their labors, and Johnny journeyed westward with them in the spring. This year a German farmer rode with him to the first camp on the Great Trail. There he meant to ask the loan of a horse for the season, and to go on alone. As room was made for him in the circle about the fire, a brave said that they had been expecting him. He pointed to the pearly crescent that hung low in the west.

"It's Johnny Appleseed moon."

There were grins at his start of surprise.

"IT'S JOHNNY APPLESEED MOON"

Yes, white settlers called him that, too. Well, that was good. It moved him profoundly to have won a nickname that stood for the faithful performance of his engagements. The Indians honored him, although they had neglected his nurseries and made little use of his ability and willingness to serve them in many practical ways. And to them he owed everything. Without their hospitality in the harder seasons and on the wilder trails his mission must have failed; and without their ponies and canoes he never could have journeyed over such great regions of country. Now they waited in silence until he had eaten of the generous bowl of hominy cooked with chestnuts and butternut meats that a squaw prepared for him, before they talked of their misfortunes.

The game was almost gone. Famine stared the children of the forest in the face. When Johnny asked if they would have food to last until the corn came in, they said that they could get what was needed at the forts in Canada. The British were their friends, and had supplied them with warm blankets and the best guns for hunting.

Johnny's heart sank with a sense of swiftly

coming disaster. There were rumors of war with England. He stood up and looked accusingly into every shifty eye.

"Where will you get skins to pay for these things? The British are bribing and arming you. If they make war on the Americans they will expect you to help them. The Americans will never be driven from the homes they have worked so hard to gain. If you are so foolish as to let yourselves be used against your neighbors you will lose all you possess. The game is gone, to return no more. Your truest friends are those who will help you get cattle, tools and seeds, and teach you the habits and tasks of white men."

Until far into the night he talked of the blessings of industry and peace. There was no famine in Piqua for Logan's tribe, which numbered seven hundred braves. In that farm village on the Miami there were warm cabins, full barns and corn-cribs, cattle in fenced pastures, meat in smoke-houses and potatoes and apples in winter pits. The squaws had spinning-wheels and looms, and in exchange for their furs the braves were buying useful tools of the Indian agent. Blackhoof, Lewis and wise old Crane, Grand

Sachem of the Wyandots, knew that this was the way of wisdom. The teachings of Tecumseh and The Prophet, that they should go to war to get back their lost lands, were evil. On what they had they could live in comfort and security.

Into that council of bitterness and despair he brought love and hope. Now he must multiply himself; engage the help of the more civilized tribes, and convert the settlers on the border to take up that heroic task of saving themselves while saving a dying race. His plans all changed, he rode away at dawn. In the waxing of his moon, and the snows and gales of early March, he went up the Cuyahoga Valley trail to Cleveland. In that region he marked trees for distribution and left supplies of seeds. Then, from the shore of Lake Erie, he turned southwest into the border trail which white men had blazed with ax-cuts on trees all the way to Dayton.

Under every rude roof that sheltered a family Johnny stopped to beg sympathy and help for the starving tribes, to warn, to reconcile. From one Indian village to another he traveled to plant seeds and to take such promise of relief as he could get. But

on both sides of the border there was much
to forgive, more to fear, and race antipathies
that no argument or appeal could break down.
And now the hunters, returning in desperate
straits, were committing fresh offenses. Johnny's apprehension and compassion for white
people and red grew, as he rode through the
misty emerald aisles of April toward Betty's
home.

Unless he made haste the orchard would
have dropped its blossoms. At sunset one
day he was still ten miles from his journey's
end, and riding so fast that he would have
overlooked a rough little black - and - white
puppy, if that wise young dog had not lain
with his keen fox nose in the path. Lamed
by a thorn in his foot, he had dropped behind
a wagon, and had waited there for hours,
confident that some one would come by who
needed a lonesome, hungry and well-inten-
tioned little dog.

Johnny picked up the waif—for he never
left a domestic animal in the woods—washed
the injured foot at a spring, shared his last
dry hoecake, and set the grateful little fellow
comfortably across his saddle-bow. It was
long after nightfall and the house was dark

when he drew rein; but a dewy incense came up from the orchard that lay in snowy drifts and mounds in the moonlighted glade.

The tall gate that opened on the trail was always padlocked at night, so he rode around the inclosure and up from the creek into the yard. He turned the horse loose in the pasture, and, not wishing to disturb the family, took his seeds and blanket to a bench under the blossoming trees. The puppy whimpering with hunger, he was obliged to go back to the spring-house to get him some milk. He was fumbling with the fastenings of the door when David called from the house:

"Who's there?"

"Johnny!"

David came out into the stoop, set his shotgun down, and shut the door behind him.

"You'd better halloo from the road after this. I might have filled you with bird-shot. Indians drove off one of my cows last week and raided the smoke-house. I'll shoot the next one that comes sneaking around my place."

"They are starving. The game is gone."

"Well, I can't feed them. They have land. Let them work as I do."

"They don't know how to work, David, and have nothing to work with. They must be helped for a long time, and be taught the simplest tasks with kindness and patience."

"You can't teach wolves to herd sheep. How are you, Johnny? Betty and the children count the days until you come." His arm went around the slender shoulders in warm affection. He fetched out a crock of milk and pushed the wagging puppy's muzzle into the creamy pool. "Stuff your skin full and grow, you little rascal. Jerusalem! Johnny, this is an English sheep-dog! He'll be as lean and swift as a hound, with a voice like a bugle and the grit to tackle his own weight in wildcats. What luck! Look here, will you?"

He unlocked the barn door and, dragging Johnny in, excitedly showed him, tied in a horse-stall, a splendid specimen of a merino ram. Napoleon had raided the flocks of Spain, and the chief duty of the United States consul at Lisbon, at that time, was buying blooded sheep for the wool-growers of New England. So serious was the need of woolen clothing in the West that men of resource and public spirit in Ohio were now bringing these valuable animals over the mountains, guarding them as they did their children, and paying bounties on wolf scalps.

"That ram came from the royal monastery of Guadeloupe, and has a pedigree as long as your arm. We call him the Little Corporal. With the ewes that Colonel Cushing is to get for me he'll cost me a quarter-section of land. What flocks we can have on these thousand hills when we get the wolves and the Indians cleaned out!"

While the door was being secured again Johnny stood with bent head. There were ten thousand warriors on the Ohio frontier, under able leadership, and driven to frenzy by suffering and evil counsel. Nothing was safe here, however so well defended by lock and gun and guardian dog.

"David, there will be war with England. Tecumseh and The Prophet are organizing and inflaming the Indians, and the British are feeding and arming them. The more civilized tribes are friendly to us, and others could be won over. We must get at that work now, this summer, while those misguided chiefs are out on the Wabash with a thousand of the most savage of the warriors—"

"General Harrison will attend to them," David interrupted, impatiently. "We might as well fight it out. If we have to lick the redcoats and the redskins both at once, why I guess we can."

"A white family has been massacred near Sandusky!"

"I know about that. Don't tell Betty. I've got an arsenal in the house, and the men of this neighborhood are building a stockade."

"Then at the first sign of trouble send Betty and the children down to Marietta. For every defenseless thing in your care you will have to answer at the bar of God."

He turned at once and went to the orchard, so heavy of heart that it was long before he slept. From dreadful dreams of the war-cry, tomahawk and torch, he woke now and then to a night that was absolutely still. The blossoming trees over which were gathering the dark clouds of savage war stood in a tranced and fragrant loveliness. Betty, coming out in a morning that was like the first that blushed on Eden, caught her breath in the sheer bliss of being alive in such a world. Johnny was asleep, and when David joined her she put her finger to her lips.

"Don't wake him. When he opens his eyes he'll look as if he thought he had died and gone to heaven."

The children tumbled out of the cabin into the happy day—Mary Lake's namesake, who was going-on-seven; David and Jonathan, the inseparable twins, and two-year-old Jimmy. Betty hushed their cries of delight over the jolly little dog, and sent them with a gourd full of wet cornmeal to feed the yellow balls of peepy chickens.

"Mary," she said in the quaint phrase that the motherly little girl had adopted, and that had won for her the nickname of Mary-go-'round, "you go 'round, dear, and look after brother Jimmy."

She hurried through her morning's work, and got out the supply of new clothing that she managed always to have ready for the beloved wanderer. Then, while he still slept she refilled his food-pouch, for he was liable to be off before any one was stirring in the morning. Fetching the low rocking-chair from the house, she sat under a tent of blossoming boughs with a bit of sewing, and watched him with the solicitude of the child of the cove of near a dozen years before.

Tears filled her eyes. All over Ohio families would be out, to-day, under the orchards he had planted, while Johnny was homeless. And he was beginning to look—not old, for he was only thirty-six, and he would have a certain look of youth if he lived to be a hundred—but marked with his years of toil and solitude, worn, purified by self-sacrifice, the gentle and ardent spirit shining through. No one in the region ever spoke of him except with tender reverence. It was a new miracle that, defenseless, he had never been in serious danger from man or beast or the elements, in a vast wilderness that bristled with perils. Just now his face was shadowed by some anxiety so deep that it pursued him into his troubled dreams. He woke with a start.

For a moment of bewilderment he thought himself back in the Pittsburg orchard on that far-away morning. Here was the rosy foam of apple-blossoms, the murmur of bees, the lilt of bird-song, the rumble of a caravan on the road; and in the little rocking-chair the appealing guest? No, he had found her grave by a deserted cabin, and had planted an apple-tree where she lay dead from an unhelped child birth, with the babe on her breast. This was Betty, and she was say-ing:

"Johnny, do you remember the night Aunt Mary Lake died? There was no one in the world then, belonging to me. And now I have David, and my arms full of darling little children, and you are here on this morning when the home you made for us all is so beautiful that I never want to go away to heaven."

"It will be like this on the other shore, Betty." He quoted from his new gospel: "For every wayside rose there is a rose idea that blooms beside the River of Life."

She placed his breakfast before him on a small rustic table, and when she sat down again she folded the useful hands that were so seldom idle. The mother of four children, she was only twenty-five, and she had the light, quick step, the merry laugh and the ready blush and tears of a girl. They had so many thoughts and memories in common, and there was only this one day in the year in which to share them.

"You remember what Dr. True used to say, Johnny, 'People can be sick any time, but my apple-tree blooms but once a year.'

There are such a lot of things to be done, but I am not going to do them to-day."

In the happy hours that followed Johnny went about the orchard pinching back buds, removing suckers, cutting out superfluous and aspiring twigs, to keep the trees headed low and open to the sun. He got a scythe and mowed the grass, and told Betty not to have it raked away. It would soon disappear in the new growth, and as it decayed something from it would be washed into the soil that would paint the fruit in the colors of ruby and gold.

"There will be company this afternoon, Johnny. We have a party every day while the trees are in bloom. People come miles from the new, bare clearings. I've made a bushel of maple sugar and nut cookies. On Sunday we'll have church. David reads from the Bible, and we sing the old hymns."

She asked Johnny to bring out the big table so they could have dinner in the orchard.

"It was Mrs. Blennerhasset who taught us the pleasure of eating out of doors. We used to row down to Isle le Beau to have strawberries and cream on the lawn. Used to! Oh, Johnny, I can't believe that our dear

Queen of the Fairy Isle has been gone five years, and is poor and in dreadful trouble. Do people blame them for being mixed up in Aaron Burr's treason?"

"No, Betty. Every one who knew them is sorry they were deceived and ruined. The island is still theirs. They should come back and live among the friends who love and trust them."

"We never could understand it. Burr was under the cloud of the duel with Hamilton, and had used and betrayed old friends before he came out to Marietta. But he dazzled every one with his plan for a colony far down the Mississippi that was to make poor settlers rich. You know how generous the Blennerhassets were. He got them to use their money to build a fleet of boats at Marietta, and to outfit them for what was a treasonable military expedition. Then warrants were out. Mr. Blennerhasset and hundreds of young men had to fly. A search party went over to Isle le Beau. Drunken militia from Virginia camped on the lawn, tore up the gardens, wrecked the furnishings, and even shot holes through the hall ceiling into Mrs. Blennerhasset's bedroom, to try

to frighten her into betraying her husband.
Colonel Cushing got a flatboat and smuggled
her and the children away on a bitter December night. What misery! And the author of
it all was never punished."

This was a thing upon which Johnny had
often pondered. The wicked had fled when
no man pursued.

"Yes, Betty, he is being punished every
hour. He is living in exile, despised and forsaken. Stripped of friends, honor and opportunity, his life can end only in poverty
and neglect. It must be punishment enough
for a man of evil and selfish ambitions to fail,
and then to have to live out the length of his
days in his own company."

"Oh, that is true!" She listened as to the
voice of some old Hebrew prophet. And as
she never had before, she understood Johnny's compensation. He might dwell with the
beasts of the fields, but in what blessedness
and peace he would live with himself to the
end! Presently she asked: "The house—that
fairy palace? Is it gone, too?"

"No, that looks much the same from Belpré. A man from Kentucky rents the farm
from Colonel Cushing, and comes with slaves

every summer to grow a crop of hemp. But from October to April the place is deserted. Parties of young people still go over to gather the nuts."

"I wish Mrs. Blennerhasset could know that. She was so good to us—so eager to give us pleasure. I am keeping the May-queen gown she gave me for my wedding, for Mary. Johnny, I wish we could take the children to the island. They cannot go into the forest here; but there, with no wild animals larger than squirrels, they could wander all day."

That island of refuge! There in the wave-washed woods of Isle le Beau, where Indians never stopped, was a place of safety for flying people for whom there would not be room in the few, small forts.

When Betty went into the house to prepare dinner, Johnny was reminded by coaxing voices and tugging little hands that it was time to go 'round the world. This was a custom begun when Mary was two years old. With the littlest baby on his back, Johnny always took them around the high-walled home-world of several acres, showed them wonders that no one else could find,

and brought them back to mother in an
hour.

There was a ruby-throat among the honeysuckles that clambered over the stoop, inquiring about when there would be coral
flagons of nectar. Although few were in
bloom, Johnny named and described the coming blossoms of the flowering annuals that
bordered the graveled path to the spring-
house. Water gurgled about the milk and
butter crocks. It would talk and laugh and
play leap-frog all the long way to the ocean.
Minnows darted in the pool. A toad hopped
out, blinking, from under the willows. A big
green frog went "plunk!" into the creek under
a sparkling fountain of spray. The trees,
the flocks of fleeces in the blue sky, the ferns
that fringed the bank, and even the children
all stood on their heads in the water.

They stalked the troops of fairies who lived
in the ferns, but those gay and clever little
people were not to be caught. Then on all-
fours, like bear cubs, they went around the
picket-fence equator, under a tangle of shrubbery that was full of nests. They saw a chip-
munk, and then they didn't, so quick that
they batted their eyes. They listened at the

grass-ball nest of a field-mouse that was packed with squeaking babies no bigger than bumblebees. There were armored and skurrying little beetles, furry pussies of caterpillars that stopped to have their backs stroked, and garden spiders spinning their fairy wheels. And up above, from Johnny's shoulder, another world was to be seen that was all flowers and butterflies.

For a long time they sat on the grass in the orchard and watched the bees visiting the apple-blossoms, and carrying their bags of honey home through the tiny doors of their street of straw hives. The chicken-yard had to have a call, and every one took turns in the swing under the arbor of fox-grapes. Johnny had a lump of salt in his pocket to coax the cows to the bars, so the calves could be petted, and apples for his horse that was resting in the pasture.

The Little Corporal had a high-fenced inclosure to himself, and for all his royal state bleated like a lamb in his lonely exile. They stayed there a long time to comfort him with handfuls of clover. Then, squealing like the fat little pink-and-white pigs in the pen, they scrambled through a plumed and tufted

hedge of lilacs and snowballs. They had a
drink from the mossy, splashy bucket at the
well, under pink banners of apple bloom, and
there they were at the stoop again. It was
noon by the mark on the new floor of broad,
white maple boards, and mother was blowing a beautiful blast on the horn to call
father from some place outside the world to
a picnic dinner.

In the afternoon they were all out in the
orchard, the children romping with the
puppy on the grass, Betty shamelessly idle,
and Johnny, propped on his elbows, reading
from his other book, or just listening to the
talk and laughter. How beautiful it was—
how peaceful and sweet, this little tiring-
room of Paradise where a happy family was
having a foretaste on earth of the joys of
eternity. It seemed incredible that this
lovely and innocent sanctuary should ever
be violated by the passions of men.

By and by a neighbor whose new cabin
stood in a snake-fenced, stump-littered clearing two miles away, was left at the gate by
her husband on his way to the mill. Mary,
who was always bursting with eager friend-
liness, reached up a plump little hand.

"Don't you want to go 'round with me and Johnny?"

"No, dear. Miz Varnum, if you don't mind, ma'am, I'd just like to set and look a spell. Them apple-trees air mighty han'-some."

Johnny told her that there would be trees in the nursery down the creek bank that David would select and help them to set out properly in the fall. Betty promised to save flower and garden seeds for her. When other visitors came she and Mary served the cookies, and spicy, pink sassafras tea in the blue cups in the orchard.

Before sundown the guests were gone. The children were fed and tucked into trundle-beds in the wing that had been added to the cabin. The still and odorous dusk folded softly like a perfumed garment about that little home of peace and love.

David came in from the fields. While Betty moved about busily in the firelight, getting supper, he began, with absorbed pleasure in the task, the serious education of the sheep-dog. First he must have a name, and learn to obey instantly when called. With duties around the imperial person of the Little

Corporal, it was found that no name would do but Old Guard. David remarked that he must go out after supper to put the ram in the barn and lock the gate.

They were at the table, which was spread with every kind of good food that a well-kept farm afforded, when an old Indian, a figure of ferocity that was like an apparition from Johnny's dreams of horror of the night, appeared at the open door and demanded something to eat.

"Get out!" David jerked a horse-pistol from the chimney-shelf. The Indian did not move, but glared hungrily at the table.

They were all on their feet. Betty had gone white and trembling, but pity was stronger than fear.

"David, won't you let me give the poor old man something? Please, dear."

"That dirty, drunken savage! Sit down, Betty. Get out! Begone with you!"

Johnny burned with sorrow and indignation. Here, in the last extremity, was the Shawnee brave who had loaned him the beautiful painted canoe, made of birch-bark from the far shores of Lake Huron, for his first voyage down the Muskingum. There was no time to use this personal plea now, but only for the soft answer.

"He may be drunk, David, but he is starving, too, and dangerous as a wolf." He turned to the Indian and tried to reach the crazed brain by speaking in the man's own dialect. "Black Arrow, you know me—Logan's brother. I have slept with you under one blanket. I have food in my pouch. Go up to the trail and I will fetch it to you."

In the delirium of the famished the man only stared at him, drew his knife and lurched toward the table. David fired. The savage turned then and staggered out of the house, to be lost at once in the dense shadows of the shrubbery. The children, startled from sleep by the shot, ran from their beds. Betty was down on the hearth with them, hushing their frightened crying.

As in a nightmare it seemed to take hours to find and light a lantern. When Johnny and David stood on the stoop with the door shut behind them, the silence of the soft spring night was stabbed through and through with a single, piteous bleat.

THE HOME ON THE BORDER

The Indian lay dead in the sheep-pasture. Beside him was his wet knife, and the Little Corporal with a dark stream flowing from the wound in his neck.

VIII

TRAGEDY

AFTER the outbreak of the early spring the Indians fell into a sullen apathy from which it was difficult to arouse them. All summer Johnny labored among them in a spiritual atmosphere that was like a hot and humid day. But, living in large groups as they did, it was easier to help them than to serve the same number of scattered white people.

To settlements as distant as Marietta he sent Logan for cattle, seeds and plows; and Piqua supplied teachers who could turn furrows, yoke oxen, make harnesses of ropes and rawhide, and build rail fences and corn-cribs. Then, as the corn ripened, the outlook became brighter. In October there was better feeling, and more food stored for winter in the Indian country of northwestern Ohio, than for many a year. No fresh reports of trouble had come from the Wabash Valley, where Tecumseh and The Prophet had their armed camp to defend the lands of the Miamis from a proposed government survey. His heart high with hope of better days Johnny made a last round of the new nurseries and then went east with the hunters.

The battle of Tippecanoe was forced by General Harrison at an opportune moment in November. But so long did it take news to travel from Indiana Territory that Pittsburg did not hear of the event for a month. With that came word of the violent and continued earthquake shocks in the Mississippi and Ohio valleys. The Prophet seized upon these disturbances to enrage the superstitious Indians. His frenzied eloquence filled the woods with painted runners to the Gulf, to dance the Lakes dances and inflame tribes to fight for their lost lands.

Johnny was then far up the Allegheny Valley, struggling through the drifted glens to reach the cider - mills, and heard nothing of these menacing matters until he brought in his seeds. The band that he joined on the Great Trail had dwindled to a dozen discouraged old men. The young braves had gone back early in the winter to take part in whatever exciting business was afoot. So far as they knew, the explosion had spent itself, and there would be no war unless the British gave the word.

The night was sharp and clear when he lay down by the camp-fire for a few hours of much-needed sleep. But suddenly they all sprang to their feet in alarm. The stars had vanished, and the hushed air was filled with a suffocating, sulphurous vapor that made the flames shoot up in long streamers and burn blue. Then the earth heaved with a vast but gentle movement, as if sighing in its sleep. Trees crashed all around the camp, a mile of caving bank thundered into the creek, and water swept in a storm-lashed flood across a marsh to their feet. Wolf-packs howled, and flying clouds of water-fowl screamed in the awful darkness. It was as if all nature was in a state of dissolution.

No shock had been felt so far east before. This lasted less than a minute, but it transformed the Indians into such primitive humans of brute fear and ferocity, with contorted limbs and bloodshot eyes, as must have inhabited an antediluvian world of monsters. For an hour they went through horrid rites to appease the anger of the Great Spirit. And even more deeply was Johnny shaken. What times were these—what portents of disaster!

He had long believed that one who lives in solitude and self-denial might see heavenly visions, and have that speech with angels which is heard within. Now, as he lay wide-eyed in the restored tranquility of the night, lifting up his heart in prayer for guidance, he thought he saw Mary Lake—not here in this wild camp, but in Betty's distant home, bending over Betty's bed. Then, a wraith-like shape that wavered in a bleak wind, she opened the door and called—the old signal for help in the emergencies of sickness—and from that dim room behind her came the sound as though a frightened child sobbed in her sleep.

Johnny roused the Indians. He had had a message and must go at once. They must take his seeds to Chief Crane at Sandusky, and let him have their best pony and a package of warrior's bread. In a quarter of an hour he was riding in midnight darkness over the Great Trail. After crossing the Muskingum, and with only a pocket compass for a guide, he plunged into the trackless forest. It was after nightfall of the fourth day that he dropped from the spent and mired pony at the door.

Within the lighted house Old Guard whined to be let out on this intruder. He leaped like a wolf, and had to be called off, when Betty let Johnny in. She stood there alone with a shotgun that fell from her shaking hands.

"You frightened me. I thought it was an Indian. So—so foolish of me. The Indians are so quiet now that David went down to Chillicothe. He has raised a militia company, and will get his captain's commission from Governor Meigs."

At once she was all concern for Johnny, fetching dry socks for his half-frozen feet, and a bowl of hot mush and milk. He asked the usual questions about the children, who were asleep, and then waited in silence for her to recover her self-control. In mending the fire she stooped with such difficulty that he took the tongs from her. At that she dropped to the hearth, and against his knees sobbed out the terror that had broken her courage.

"D-David wouldn't have left me for that—now. He was obliged to go, to—to fetch a doctor—to help me. We didn't think—I'd need help—so soon. I cried for Aunt Mary Lake. She'd come if she could, Johnny. I was afraid I might die—and the children be left here—alone."

"She called me!" His voice was hushed with the wonder and glory of the vision that had brought him here. He told Betty about it as he lifted her to the bed. "I am going back to a sugar-camp to get an Indian woman. Dr. True says that some old squaws can beat him at this kind of big medicine. Old Guard is a regiment in himself. He knew before he was born that it would be his duty to protect something. Put up the bars and go to sleep."

On the return journey the horse that he took from the stable carried double. The ancient and hideous dame had come unwillingly, and only on the promise of a horse-load of potatoes, pork and apples; but when she saw Betty her black eyes sparkled with professional pride, and she spoke tenderly enough in her soft Shawnee tongue.

"Pretty squaw! Her all right now."

Johnny was glad that there were things to be done—animals to be fed, cows to be milked, wood and water to be fetched, and scared children to be reassured, kept out of doors and told something of the sacred mystery of birth.

"You must be quiet and happy. There's a little angel hovering over this house, trying to come down to earth to be a brother or sister to you. Mother will be in there, waiting, until God lays the darling little bit of a baby in her arms."

After an Indian camp-fire dinner in the barn-lot, and a romp in the haymow, the three little boys went to sleep and Mary covered them warm with the sweet-smelling hay. Leaving Old Guard on duty, she and Johnny went a half-mile down the creek to the nursery. To the child who could count on her dimpled fingers the few times that she had been taken out of the home inclosure, this was thrilling adventure. Back from the gravelly margin of the stream stretched a flood bank that was covered with a low growth of leafless willows and alders, and last year's tall, rusty ferns. The thicket closed behind them, and left no trace of their passage when they crossed it to the higher ground that sloped steeply up to the forest-screened trail.

In a natural, under-washed bend of the bluff, and behind a tall, stake-and-brush fence that was woven with the living cables of fox-grapes, the nursery was concealed from all but its canopy of gray sky. Bursting with delight, but noiselessly as any squirrel, for Johnny had whispered that this was a secret place, Mary scrambled up the stout trellis and dropped near orderly rows of apple-twigs. In every settled district in Ohio Johnny now had these forest fastnesses, of which the Indians knew nothing, where flying people might find temporary safety. He had a purpose in bringing the child here, but must not frighten her.

"Mary-go-'round, father knows about this, but might not think of it, or be at home when— Tell mother what a fine place it is for hiding, so if she ever wanted to take you all away—in a hurry—"

Mary nodded with gay understanding. To a child it is the happy impulse of any moment to want to go somewhere else in a hurry. She would never have her mother's delicate beauty nor the gentle sweetness that won the heart and made it ache. But a friendly, helpful, cheerful little person in a brown, butternut-dyed cloak, squirrel-skin hood, and red knitted stockings and mittens, she flitted about like a winter robin while Johnny went over the ground foot by foot, to make sure there were no snake-holes.

The squaw was gone when, on the third day, David burst into the house with an ashen face and hoarse voice. "The Indians have broken out again. The woods are full of murdering bands. Fetch the children!"

He wrapped Betty and the day-old babe that lay on her breast in the bed-clothing, swept them up into his arms, and raced down the frozen lawn to the creek bank. While the children were scrambling into outer garments, Johnny ran with the bearskin rugs, to be laid in the rowboat and over mother and child. Mary sat by them to keep the coverings tucked in, and David took the oars. Johnny followed in the big canoe with the little boys and Old Guard.

Torn veils of fine, dry snow streamed before a westerly wind that sent them scudding down the swollen creek. In an hour they reached the stockade in a tiny settlement on the Scioto, into which frantic people were gathering. Johnny helped carry Betty up the bluff and into a blockhouse, where she would at least have the care of women. No doctor could be spared from the small capital, where there was much sickness. As long as he lived he never forgot how she lay with the wee, downy face of the gasping infant pressed to her breaking heart.

He had left her—to suffer this. How would it be with him if she perished?

He spent a week driving down cows and taking boat and wagon loads of provisions to the log fort. David remained in command, and half the men returned to cultivate the fields and protect the deserted homes. A few were shot from ambush at their plows; horses and cattle were run off, and some cabins and orchards burned. Betty's baby died from the exposure, and Johnny buried it under the apple-tree with the low, roomy crotch, where she could have the sad comfort of seeing the short, grassy mound from the doorway. The coming struggle was claiming its first, innocent victims.

War was not yet a certainty, and was, in-

deed, not declared until the middle of June;
but troops had been ordered to proceed to
Dayton in May, to impress the Indians and
to prepare the Northwest for defense. Johnny went up to Sandusky for his seeds, and
spent the next six weeks in Indian villages
where no work was being done.

In the outbreak of early winter even
peaceful and industrious tribes had reverted
to savagery, broken their plows and looms,
eaten their seed for this year's crops, and
slaughtered their cattle for horrid feasts.
Now they repented in a bitter poverty that
was relieved only by thieving raids across
the border. Other tribes Johnny found in
the brief enjoyment of a dreadful prosperity.
The braves had new blankets and firearms,
and their villages were abundantly supplied
with beef and flour. He rebuked them for
their treacherous folly, and refused to eat
anything of theirs except the forest nuts, and
the corn they had grown with their own
honest labor.

The orchards that he had planted—apple-
trees whose ripening fruits would be roasted
on their living branches—were in blossom
when, as if some secret word was borne on

the wind, the braves went westward. In a
week not a warrior was to be seen east of the
Miami, and the border settlers returned to
their homes. Since nothing would be planted
that year but men, no harvests gathered besides souls. Johnny rode out to Piqua, where
Logan had his seven hundred warriors under
arms to defend his village and the American
trading-post. Going on down to Dayton,
he sent his seeds and tools to Cincinnati,
to be forwarded to Colonel Cushing at
Belpré, and then turned to the work of re-
lieving suffering.

The outlook was appalling. Of the army
that was gathering, only one regiment was
United States regulars. The young pioneers
of the Ohio militia and volunteers were wholly
untrained, and were led by self-chosen officers, and they came in the poor clothing that
they had worn at their work in field and
forest. They brought their own arms:
cheap shotguns, rusty muskets and rifles that
their fathers had used in Mad Anthony's
campaign of eighteen years before, and even
some flintlocks—sacred relics of the Revolu-
tion. Blacksmiths came up from Cincinnati
to mend these worthless weapons, and farmers

molded bullets and emptied their powder-
horns to supply ammunition. Johnny nursed
the sick, for teeth were chattering with ague,
and he scoured the country for blankets and
shoes, corn and pork.

Yet this feeble force of five thousand men,
under the leadership of a Revolutionary vet-
eran who was in his dotage, was expected to
cut its way through two hundred miles of
Indian - owned forests to Detroit, with five
times its number of perfectly equipped savages hanging on the flanks and waiting for
orders from British officers in Fort Malden.

A cry of fury and despair went up from the
poor and scattered settlers on a long frontier,
a cry for an army and supplies adequate to
the task, with their own Indian - fighter,
General Harrison, in command. But Washington was far away, and the peril of the border but an incident to a nation unprepared.
After gun and torch and tomahawk had ravaged the country to the Ohio River, the Old
Northwest must defend itself, find the men
and money, train its own leaders, and build
its own fleet of green timber on Lake Erie.

There was one thing that these young
pioneers knew how to do supremely—how to

fell trees, and with them build blockhouses and log bridges, and lay the swamps with corduroy. When the word was given the axes rang up the valley of the Miami. Johnny found Captain Varnum leading his company in a mighty slaughter of ancient timber, and learned that Betty and the children were on the farm. Neighbors were caring for the corn and cattle. When the fighting began they would go down to Marietta.

"I'll be where the earliest news is to be had, and alarm the people along the border if there is need," Johnny reassured him.

There was a wild hurrah of relief and pride when word went abroad that the gallant boys had cut their way into Detroit. With such a feeling of security as the Northwest had not had in a year and a half, men returned to their corn-fields, never dreaming that this strong key-fortress could be so speedily lost.

But Johnny knew. An amazing mistake had been made. At the rapids of the Maumee, finding the march through the woods hampered by the transport of supplies, the food, military stores and medicines were loaded on a sailing-vessel and sent by water. The exhausted troops dropped in the barracks

within the gates, only to learn that war had
been declared and that the boat had been
captured by the British on Lake Erie. A
small force of Ohio volunteers was sent back
at once to the vine-clad banks of the River
Raisin to meet and protect the reinforcements
and supplies that had been started north.
This was ambushed by a band of Tecumseh's
warriors who slipped over from Canada.

At this news, which struck consternation
to the hearts of the defenders, Johnny sought
the colonel of the Third Ohio Volunteers.
A man seven years younger than himself,
Lewis Cass had come out to Marietta in the
same year, to study law with Governor Meigs
and then to ride the Muskingum Valley cir-
cuit. Even at thirty he was a ponderous
young man of heavy figure and large, smooth-
shaven, immobile face. His words were few
and well considered, and he had a reputation
for honesty, solid learning, clear thinking,
and a quiet, constructive patriotism that
must lead to some distinguished service. It
was the future Governor who was destined
to transform the wilderness of Michigan Territory into a modern state who answered
Johnny's question with deliberation.

TRAGEDY

"A criminal blunder has been committed, and we must pay for it. It will take two years to overcome the mistake. Get out, Johnny, and save all the people you can."

When Captain David Varnum marched with the second relief party out of the beleaguered fortress, Johnny disappeared in the woods to learn what he could of the enemy's plans from the native Indians. At Brownstown he found a village of friendly Wyandots, whose young braves were out warning the scattered families of French trappers and scouting for the American army. If the fort was surrendered they were to take the news to the valleys of the Maumee, Miami and Wabash. Thence it could be carried swiftly to Dayton and Vincennes. With the Ohio border this tribe was unacquainted, and they could not, in any case, reach it in time.

"Why?" Johnny was startled.

Chief Walk-in-the-Water drew a map of the head of Lake Erie in the ashes. Word of a British and Indian victory would be carried by canoe to Sandusky. From there the runners would scatter, small bands striking the border at many points at once. Killing and burning everything in their path, they

would make for the crossing-places of the
Ohio River, and stir up tribes to war from
Michigan to Alabama. Braves from San-
dusky were with Tecumseh.

"I cannot believe that!" cried Johnny.
"Chief Crane is a stanch friend of the Americans, and a wise and honest man."

There was a shrug. The Grand Sachem
was old. Many evil things were done under
his nose, and to much that he saw he shut
his eyes, for he could no longer hold the hot-
heads of his tribe who were all for war. No
doubt ample means for carrying out this plot
were hidden near his village.

"Then I must find and destroy them."

With a bag of parched corn for food, and
a horse that knew the narrow trace through
the jungle of the Black Swamp which stretched
from the Maumee to the Sandusky River,
Johnny slipped around the deserted shore of
the lake. Making a detour of the populous
Indian town, he camped in the edge of the
woods on a sandy point that overlooked the
wide entrance to the bay. Night after night,
in the light of the full moon, when the forest
was peopled with a host of shifting shadows
and one more could pass unnoticed, he crept

down - shore. Near the landing - place and around the village he searched the brush-grown hollows until he found the unopened cases of firearms and ammunition. Not knowing how much time he would have, and frantic with fear for the thousands of imperiled people, it was all he could do to wait for the dark of the moon. Then paddling cautiously out in a canoe, he dropped the guns in deep water. The powder he emptied in bog-holes and covered with muck, and to the thirsty sand he gave the kegs of fire-water.

There was more that he failed to find; but the loss of so much would alarm and delay the runners, and he dared not risk discovery. Moving several miles to the east, he lay hidden on the lake-shore trail, with his horse saddled and tethered in a grassy glade, while he lived on parched corn and wild black-berries. In the long hours of watching he worked out the details of the feat of Logan who, unaided, had fetched twenty-five white women and children out of Fort Wayne and down through a hundred miles of forest swarming with hostile savages, in safety, to Piqua. There was more than a chance that he could do that. Like the foxes of the hills, in whose dens he had slept, he knew the twists and turns and secret retreats of every wild way in Ohio.

The year declined from the zenith and drowsed through the long days of August. At four o'clock in the morning the disk of the dog-star burned like a little moon above the silvery expanse of the most placid of all the Great Lakes. At noon the sun shimmered on a blue field that was seldom ruffled by storm; and it set late, in splendor, behind the violet islands. Sixteen hours a day Johnny watched those low, wooded masses and rocky headlands. In crossing this wide body of water Indians rested midway, and when the weather was clear a camp-fire could be seen, like a flickering red star, low down on the water. But men who turn into demons and run on the devil's errands stop for nothing. It was out from under a rising morning mist that an enormous fleet of canoes appeared and sped toward the bay. As they neared the shore the reckless braves stood up and waved their arms in the contortions of the primitive war-dance. Some leaped overboard and swam to the landing.

Detroit had surrendered!

TRAGEDY

Johnny dashed into the woods and leaped to the saddle. By riding south, straight down the Scioto trail, he could make sure of rescuing Betty and her children. But if he did that the scattered settlers along the lake shore, and the many people on the nearer border for a hundred miles southwestward from Cleveland, would have no warning. Massacre unchecked would run red to the Great Crossing of the Muskingum.

Digging the only pair of spurs he ever owned into the flanks of the horse, he galloped east. All day he pounded through heavy sands and struggled across the wide, marshy mouths of the innumerable waterways. At isolated cabins standing in corn-fields and orchards he called out his message. It was dusk when his horse fell dead before a door where a family ran out from a rude supper-table at his shout:

"Detroit has fallen! Indians coming! Keep off the trails! Warn your neighbors! Take the news to Cleveland! A horse and food!"

From a fresh mount he drank a gourd of milk. A woman stuffed his pockets with hoe-cakes. In five minutes he was gone into the twilight aisles of the border trail. Thundering through the sloughs, and up and down the undulations of the watershed, he blew blasts from a sawed-off powder-horn that could be heard a mile. With his trumpet-call, which sounded like the day of judgment, he aroused cabins and settlements where people slept with their doors open in the stifling heat of the August night. Into the darkness and into the ghostly light of a late-rising moon they sprang from their beds. Many began to harness their oxen and horses to old caravans, and to bring out their household goods, but Johnny cried:

"Fly at once! Take what food you can, and pile onto your horses! Turn your cattle and pigs loose in the woods! Hide the women and children in the nursery until the Indians have passed! The men must stay out to warn every family they can reach! Then make for the nearest stockade through the wildest glens and swamps! If that is crowded, go by night marches, afoot, to the Ohio River!"

On through the short summer night he rode. In the earliest hours in the morning his horse flagged in his pace. He dragged

TRAGEDY

the saddle off and turned the animal into a
grassy glade to give him a chance of life.
At the next cabin, a mile away, he captured
a half-broken colt in a pasture. His ears

HE BLEW BLASTS FROM A SAWED-OFF POWDER-HORN
THAT COULD BE HEARD A MILE

ringing with screams, a panorama of horror-stricken faces swimming before his eyes, he raced on.

He saw the sick carried from their beds, and he herded families that, in the moment of panic, would have scattered. In an orchard, her apron full of windfalls, he found a half-foolish and palsied grandmother who had been forgotten. Sweeping her up to the saddle, he restored her to the distracted family. At a log mill he ran into a dozen farmers who were waiting for their grist, ten and twenty miles from their homes. Paralyzed for a moment by his message, they stood like dead trees, then leaped to their horses and fled.

In the middle of the second night he heard yells and saw the smoky flare of pine-knot torches. A bullet whistled by his head, and his colt leaped as if shot and sped like an arrow. Rising in the stirrups, Johnny gave the war-whoop to deceive the Indians into thinking him one of themselves. Cold sweat burst from every pore. Massacre and burning had overtaken him! In a dawn of rose and gold and amethyst he passed a cabin whose smoldering ruin was ringed with charred corn. Slain animals lay on the ground, but by some miracle the people had escaped. But looking down a small waterway he heard triumphant yells and saw a great volume of fiery smoke billow up from the woods.

At that he reeled in his saddle and ceased to think. He was still a trumpet-call—a voice crying in a wilderness of nameless horrors—but his mind was lifted above conscious thought in one wild prayer for Betty and her little brood. In this hour of anguish he remembered the pallid face and wide blue eyes that the war-orphaned child of the cove above the shipyard at Marietta had turned upon him. Now, in tortured fancy, he saw her so again, but lying among the ferns on the creek bank, staring up at God.

It was true that her home lay on the Piqua trail, twenty miles within the border; but the beautiful place was widely known, and even in the first rush the Indians would go out of their way to destroy it. Every farm that he passed had been swept by fire, and ghastly shapes lay on the ground. And now another messenger was abroad—smoke. In the dead air of a day of humidity heavy vapors were unable to rise above the canopy of the forest. The vistas were blue with the suffocating cloud, and flights of complaining wood-pigeons streamed out to the clearer air of the hilltops.

He had turned eastward on the long home-stretch when he overtook Logan on horseback with his ten-year-old daughter Ellen on a pony. Not knowing that Detroit had surrendered the chief had left Piqua two days before to take this child, who was the apple of his eye, to Chillicothe out of the perils of savage warfare. From there he meant to send her on to the family of his foster-father, Captain Logan, near Lexington, Kentucky. Now he transferred her to Johnny's care.

"My wife will not leave her people, and the lads are braves who must share the fate of their tribe. Nelly will not delay you. She can ride as hard and fast as you. Take her on with you and save your friends. I will ride down the border to Dayton."

"Have you heard anything of Captain Varnum?"

"Fell in a second ambush on the River Raisin."

TRAGEDY

They gripped hands with the sense of loss which comes from a last parting.

As they separated the dark father and child faced each other. "Farewell, Nelly. The lodge will be lonely without you. Love your new home and friends. Grow up white." Their looks clung to each other until the chief wheeled and galloped away. Their next meeting was in the land of the Great Spirit, for Logan was killed in the following year when scouting for General Harrison. If this little royal exile shed a tear, now, no one knew. Burying her face in the pony's long mane she raced after Johnny.

Along the smoke-dimmed, winding trail the endless lines of motionless trees made the shadowy, inescapable walls of a labyrinth seen in a nightmare. The sun had begun to decline when Johnny swayed dizzily on smelling burned wood and roasted apples. His horse shied and bolted, leaving him on the wreckage of the wagon-gate of Betty's home. Within the circle of blasted orchard trees the field-stone chimney stood above the dying embers of the house.

IX

THE SAVIOR OF THE REFUGEES

OLD GUARD shot out of the thicket on the flood bank when Johnny ran down the creek, leaped ferociously, and then fawned upon him in frantic delight and raced back to the nursery. Johnny put his lips to the close-woven, leafy screen.

"Betty! Are you all there? Safe?"

His knees gave way under him when he heard the breath of a reply. On the other side he knew that she too knelt, thanking God that he was here. After a moment he was able to whisper:

"Wait. There are some things I must do."

He gave the whinnying pony a slap on the flank that sent him flying across the water and into the woods. No grazing animal could starve, and in summer it was not likely to be

198

attacked by wolves. Then he turned to the painted savage who lay not a hundred yards away, a ghastly thing with his throat torn open by Old Guard, and dragged the body into the densest part of the undergrowth. Washing the dog's bloody muzzle in the creek, he bade him run up the slope and jump into the inclosure. Scrambling over the swaying trellis, he pulled Ellen up after him.

Betty was crouched with the children in the cave-like hollow at the back, behind the plantation of apple-twigs. Out of her drawn and colorless face her heavily ringed eyes stared like the unseeing eyes of the dead. But for her terror-stricken little people there was merciful diversion in the Indian maid. A gorgeous tropical bird dropping from the sky could not have astonished them more. In her petticoat of crimson cloth, her elaborately beaded moccasin-leggings of deerskin, and the jaunty blue jacket that dripped silver buttons, she looked to be all that Johnny described her.

"This is Princess Nelly Logan, of Piqua."

Nothing but friendly and admiring looks greeted the forlorn and blameless child; but the Princess Nelly shrank back. She had seen such things as must make white people turn with horror from one of her race. With the face of a stone image, but a heaving breast, she stood aloof until Mary-go-'round ran and laid a rosy cheek against her own of warm bronze.

"I never had a sister. Let's be twin sisters."

"All right." There was a tear that Mary kissed away. The two little girls lay down together on a bed of leaves in the cave, with their arms around each other like the babes in the woods, when Johnny whispered that they must all go to sleep at once, so they would be rested for travel at night. When he went back to the screen with the sentinel dog, Betty followed him.

"What—what has happened?"

"Detroit has fallen."

With a choking sound she swayed against him. A question about David was on her blue lips, but she forbore to ask it, and Johnny did not tell her. She could bear no more, and would need all the hope and courage she could keep to sustain her in the terrible days to come. At this moment her distracted mind must be turned into safer channels.

"Dear Betty, think of the children you must help me save, and try to sleep," he begged. But when, staggering from the exhaustion of he knew not how many hours of waking, he fell in a limp heap at her feet, he knew that she would sit there beside him, shuddering, all the waning afternoon. Katydids were calling across the dusk when she woke him and gave him bread and told him the brief story of their escape.

"The smoke alarmed me. Wood-pigeons streamed out, complaining, as if the whole border was on fire. Then chickens, pigs and cattle were on the trail. I sent the children on ahead. The dog drove the farm animals into the woods, and I got a basket of food and the children's shoes. We heard —things that will ring in our ears forever. When they had burned the house the Indians searched for us. And after a band went by overhead Old Guard dashed out at something—someone—"

"Don't think about it any more." The thought of the death that had almost tracked her and hers to this hiding-place turned his own heart to ashes. She did make an effort to think of other things, and pointed to the trampled nursery in mute distress. At that Johnny could find it in him to smile.

"I'm glad. Oh, I pray to God that all my nurseries may lie in ruins under the feet of people who escaped the fate of their homes and orchards."

Now they must plan what they were to do. He told her that they might not find safe shelter until they reached the Ohio. Once across the Scioto, they could make for Belpré through the wild country which lay back of the valley of the Hocking, avoiding the river, the trails and the settlements. And on their way they must rescue every one they could. While Johnny went out to find the rowboat, where it was hidden among the willows, Betty gathered up the food and knotted the children's leather shoe-strings. Then, looking at the Princess Nelly, she thought of something that would not have occurred to the wisest man.

"My dear! This will never do! Have you nothing plainer to wear?"

Few backwoods families ever had anything more than the ugliest and scantiest of clothing, and they went barefooted eight months in the year. This beautiful raiment on one

of the feared and hated race would arouse
bitter resentment, and perhaps violence, in
poor fugitives. With loving compassion she
helped the little girl into a linsey slip and
clumsy shoes, and hid the offending splendor
in the small bundle of necessaries that she
carried on her back.

Johnny had them all lie down in the boat.
Using an oar for a rudder to keep the light
craft in the shadow of the bank, he let it
drift down the dark stream. The moon would
not rise until three o'clock in the morning.
Before midnight they reached the stockade
on the Scioto. The settlement had been
burned, and the tiny fort was crowded. Many
had gone by to Chillicothe, and more were
arriving every hour. One family had been
overtaken and massacred in full view of the
gate. The bodies would have to lie out
until morning. Crying had been heard, of
a child or a panther, or perhaps an Indian to
lure rescuers to an ambush.

Telling a sentinel that he would remain
near this crossing of trails as long as people
continued to come, and save all he could,
Johnny went down. He was getting into the
boat when the sheep-dog came out of the

undergrowth with the handle of a splint basket in his mouth. Betty lifted the baby that a doomed mother had pushed into the brush as she ran, and hushed its wail of hunger with a bit of maple sugar tied up in a kerchief. For the first time in that long day of horrors she found the relief of tears.

Johnny turned the boat into the Scioto. A mile down-stream he shot it across to a point on the eastern bank where a parting of the hills was covered with small swamp-timber. In late summer the ground was nearly dry, but under the low branches of the trees it was all a tangle of pea-vines, noisome water-weeds, and thorny shrubs. In the black jungle snakes had to be risked. Taking three-year-old Jimmy on his back, and posting the dog at the rear, he broke the way to a grassy opening.

"Not here," he signaled. Plunging into the woods, he mounted a grassy rise that was covered with acres of wild grapes. The scared and weary children dropped, sobbing, in the pitch blackness of the leafy tents. Wise little Ellen Logan put her hand firmly and repeatedly over every quivering mouth, and whispered that it was dangerous to cry.

With a word of reassurance and orders to Old Guard, Johnny was gone. Making his way back to the stockade, he lay below the trail with his ear to the ground until he heard the beat of galloping hoofs and the rumble of a wagon. Pursuit was close behind this fleeing family when he sprang to the horses' heads.

"Jump out! Throw out your food!" He fairly hurled them into the brush, and lashed the horses into a run down the steep bank and across the ford. The shots that rang from the blockhouse were returned by the Indians as they dashed by and plunged into the river. In the confusion of loud noises, Johnny reached out a hand and spoke to the sturdy young German who was comforting his weeping wife.

"Hermann, take your wife and child down to the boat and stay there with them." When he had a load of rescued people he left this first man to watch the trails, and went down the river.

Betty came out of the black camp with the infant whose screams of hunger imperiled them all. "Is there a woman here with a baby? She must give one breast to this motherless child."

Dawn glimmered in the forest fastness as the third boat-load was brought in. One family had a bag of meal and a small iron kettle. A fire was built in a wild-grape tepee, and by instalments enough mush was boiled for thirty people. Remembering that farm animals were everywhere at large, Betty took Old Guard's long muzzle in her hands and looked into his intelligent eyes.

"Drive home the cows."

The sheep-dog was plainly puzzled; but presently he put his nose to the ground and trotted away. The sun was high when, with all the pride of discovery, he brought in two cows with dripping udders.

For two days and another night the women and children lay hidden, with the dog and one man to guard them, while Johnny and the other men took turns in watching the trails and scouring the woods. Every hour exhausted and half-crazed people were brought in. Some came down from the stockade, which held only a small supply of food, and was liable at any time to be attacked in force. A woman was found in a hollow tree. Two children were traced to a blackberry-patch, to which they had been led by the almost human footprints of bears.

In the wild flight naked feet had been cruelly bruised and cut, so that many could not hope to keep up on the hard night marches. Ellen helped solve that problem. Going about timidly, she bathed the wounds and bound them with cool plantain leaves. From a horse-blanket Betty cut bag moccasins with a hunting-knife, and laced them about ankles with strips from a rawhide harness. The men fashioned soles of tough beech bark, and tied them on with raveled hemp rope.

More than a hundred people followed Johnny on the first night's march down a ravine whose ribbon of bright water was arched over by phantasmal sycamores. Night after night they made their slow way over forest-clad ridges, through tangled slashings and gullies, and baffling mazes of laurel on rough hillsides. By day they camped in wild vineyards, in deep, brush-grown pockets of the hills, and in the dry beds of ponds in the middle of rustling marshes. At times warwhoops came faintly to their ears, and along some distant, elevated trail pine-knot torches glimmered like fireflies. When smoke from a burning cabin or settlement drifted over them, more people would be found huddled in a cave or in one of Johnny's nurseries.

Famine marched with them, although food was in abundance. The smallest stream had fish; the wild oats were full of quail; myriads of water-fowl skimmed every pond; and flocks of turkeys fed in the oak and chestnut groves on last year's withered acorns and nuts. But they dared not fire a rifle, nor cook any savory thing whose odor would betray them. Only in the most hidden situations, indeed, could they venture to roast the potatoes and corn which they found about the few deserted cabins that had been overlooked by the Indians. The cows that Old Guard drove in kept the children alive. Once meal was discovered in a half-burnt mill which had broken from its moorings and drifted into back-water.

A small number of people, able to scatter and move about freely by day, could have foraged for plums, beaten out the oats, and dug lily roots in the marshes. But this furtive and flying company grew to a small army, and every addition to the ranks increased the suffering and peril of all. Speech was abandoned. They fell into the silence of fortitude or listening terror, of dumb bewilderment or dull misery. Johnny had to shorten the marches. On the last night there was a journey of only a few hours to be made, but that was in the rough knobs of the Ohio River. Up and down the steep hills, densely wooded with oaks and hickories, staggering men carried limp children and fainting women supported one another. Johnny's cheering word went back to spur the falling line to another effort.

"Courage now! Almost there!"

After a terrible hour they broke through to thinner growth on the crest of a grassy, spurlike ridge. A gun-shot brought them to a standstill, with such a shock of cruel fright that women and children sank weeping to the ground.

"Halt! Who's there?" The challenge came up from below, where, at every ten rods of the three miles of rail fence which stretched along the woods at the top of the farms, Belpré had posted a sentinel.

"Johnny Appleseed with refugees."

Young Waldo Putnam ran up from the fields, and dropped his rifle when he saw that famishing host. "The Lord save us, Johnny! How are we to care for all the perishing people who are coming down upon us? Every house is full to the ridge-pole, and two hundred are living in Farmers' Castle. We have food, but no shelter."

"Is any one living on Isle le Beau?"

"Not now. You know Indians never stop there, but the tenant took his niggers and lit out for Kentucky like a scared rabbit when the first runners made the crossing."

"We'll camp in the woods on the lower end of the island."

People who had dropped were dragged to their feet again. For a mile the low ridge ran across the meadows, dividing the farm village into the upper and lower towns, and rising to a hundred-foot bluff above the water. They could hear the rustling corn and smell the laden orchards, but the scattered houses of the long street that fronted the river were dark. Johnny laid Betty in the midst of her spent children under the cedars. Almost falling down the slope in his haste and weakness, he hammered on Colonel Cushing's door.

A strange, wild figure, stricken with famine, transfigured by his errand, he was. Since he left Dayton in May he had been in the wilderness, in such stress of mind and circumstances that his dark hair had grown to his shoulders and fallen about his gaunt face. His shirt was in tatters, and because they impeded his movements he had cut his ragged trousers to the knees, exposing his scarred and swollen legs and bark-sandaled feet. The family, startled from their beds by what they thought an Indian alarm, were not certain of his identity until, with a frantic cry, he crumpled up in the doorway.

"Help for starving people in the cedar-grove on the bluff!"

Doors flew open and lights appeared. People boiled out of the houses and the timber château of Farmers' Castle like bees from hives, and swarmed on the beach. There was a confusion of shouts and running footsteps. Johnny fainted from sheer relief when he saw the huge negro, Kitt Putnam, in the van of the stalwart men who started up the bluff to carry the helpless down. When he came to himself, with his head in Mrs. Cushing's lap and a cup of warm milk at his lips, the boats and the ferry were being manned, and the young girls of Belpré, in their light summer gowns, were moving about with candles, ministering to the prostrate crowd on the sand.

It was near morning before all were got across. In the fear that some Indian might be lurking about, sentinels were posted at the landing-place. Family groups slept wherever they dropped in that woodland sanctuary —slept to waken late in the day, to be fed and comforted, and to sleep again. So the scores that Johnny had led to safety won their way back to health and sanity, and to the taking up of their broken lives.

Six weeks later he returned to Belpré. Knowing the country as did no one else, he had guided a force of armed and mounted men from the Ohio River settlements, all over the region up to Zanesville and the new town of Columbus, to relieve the beleaguered stockades, bury the dead, and round up the farm animals in the woods. It was incredible that civilized human beings would ever re-people that desolated wilderness; but no other talk was heard than to fight it out, then to go back and begin again.

Such courage and faith thrilled Johnny. With autumn colors flaming against the silvery blue of Indian-summer skies, it was seed-time, and he must be off to replant his ruined nurseries, in such wild solitude and danger as he had never faced before. Wolves would increase and become bolder. There would be no friendly faces to greet him, no sheltering cabins except in the few, defensible settlements, no Indian camps on the Great Trail. And he must stay out nine months in the year, traveling fast and incessantly, to keep his plots from being overrun with weeds and forest seedlings.

His dark-gray eyes burned with zeal when he brought Mrs. Cushing in haste to the door to assure him that his seeds and tools had come up from Cincinnati. The Princess Nelly's beautiful, long-tailed pony had been found, and Johnny ran to the mill to arrange for Kitt Putnam to be spared a week to take the chief's little daughter on in state to Kentucky. Aside from Kitt's special qualities, no escort was as safe for woman or child as a negro, upon whom the most savage Indian looked with sympathy as a dark-skinned brother of misfortune.

Colonel Cushing was drilling raw recruits on the beach—"licking these young cubs into shape so General Harrison can use 'em," he explained to Johnny. In bordering states, and in every far-flung settlement of the Old Northwest, there was grim determination to overcome this paralyzing disaster. Here in Belpré the new wheat was being ground; wheel and loom hummed and clattered in every house, and grandmothers and little girls knitted in the sun for the soldiers. Pigs were being fattened; standing corn and the recovered horses and cattle guarded in field and pasture, and potatoes and apples gathered to store in winter pits.

Never had Johnny seen such a harvest of apples. They lay in glowing heaps under the trees of three miles of almost continuous orchards, coloring the earth and perfuming the air. All the old fall and winter favorites were there—the Bellflowers and Pippins, the Greenings and Spies, the Seek-no-furthers and Never-fails, the Russets and Rambos. Very early in the last century this town, on its rich, alluvial meadow, became famous for the cargoes of fruit that it shipped to New Orleans. This crop was to have gone into the hold of the *Comet*, the amazing new steamboat that went plunging and shrieking like some fiery dragon up and down the forest-walled floods of the Ohio and Mississippi.

Johnny's instant thought was that, in the matter of orchards, the river settlements could now take care of themselves, and after the war there would be nurserymen in the larger towns. He was released to work in the backwoods. Now for an hour he gave himself up to the pleasure of strolling under the trees which were dropping their leaves in preparation for peaceful sleep, and feasting on the fruit in the company of this New-Englander of such genial and sterling virtues. They spoke of the refugees on Isle le Beau. Many had already gone on to friends, and shelter must be found for all before winter set in. As for the orphans, there would always be "room for one or two more" under Colonel Cushing's roof.

"My good wife and I are getting on in years, Johnny, but we'll take in all we can. I guess the youngsters won't mind sleeping three in a bed. There'll be a bed for you, too, if it turns my rheumatic old bones out on the floor. What will you do now?"

"Go back. Begin again."

"Hm, yes, after the war we'll all have to

begin again. Johnny, we meant to pay you for this bounty in one lump sum when we sold the surplus of this crop. Now we must keep what we have for the army and to feed homeless people. But better days are coming. When the war is over the East is going to break up and move West."

Then the eager words tumbled out: "You can pay me now with a horse, a blanket and a bag of meal. There must be orchard trees to set out when these brave people return to their fire-swept clearings. No," he interrupted the shocked protest, "I shall not starve and the Indians will not molest me. An apple-twig in his bridle protects my horse from thieves. Good-by! Unless you set up cider-mills so I can get seeds down here, I may not see you again. New-comers will pour into the Indian lands that will be forfeited or purchased now, and I must go westward on the crest of every new wave."

He gripped the hand of this long-time friend and turned away at once. So he had parted from David Varnum and Logan. So, with a sharper pang, he must part from Betty and miss from his life the little Eden that had, for so many years, been his heart's home on the border. Until the little boys grew up, he thought, she would be obliged to live in Marietta, where David's people and Dr. True would see that she lacked nothing. Except in spirit he could hold to no one. He could foresee his life as one long story of hail and farewell.

In a voice gone husky Colonel Cushing bade him Godspeed. These bowering orchards were the gift of this missionary of peace and beauty and brotherly love who had woven himself into the very fabric of their lives. Now they were losing him, and to the children of the third generation he would be a legend, his blossoming and fruiting memorials benefits forgot. With a lump in his throat and misty eyes he watched Johnny stride across the fields and beach, and launch a canoe—watched until he had leaped to the landing and disappeared among the majestic trees of Isle le Beau.

That Fairy Island! Its queen in ruined exile, her white palace stood in a stained and battered beauty. On the weedy lawn bare patches marked the bonfires of vandals. The tall picket fence of the garden was down, with its wall-fruit trees barked and dead. Behind

the classic pillars of the curving verandas
that flanked the front, baled hemp was stored,
inviting the accidental fire which destroyed
the historic mansion on the Christmas eve
of that year. Within, the wainscoted hall
had been turned into a sleeping-kennel by
black field laborers. The Cushings and Put-
nams had rescued the spinet, a portion of the
library, and much else, in a forlorn hope that
the owners would return to claim them. But
here were torn draperies hanging from broken
windows, wrecked furniture, shattered mir-
rors, wanton bullet-holes, dishonored books,
cobwebs, dust, and the dissolution that comes
to the house untenanted.

At the end of the two-mile walk across the
pastures and up through the woods he found
Betty sitting on a fallen log, directing a group
of women in cutting and sewing new garments. In a secret closet of Mrs. Blennerhasset's big garret workroom, where her free
black servants had spun and wove and fashioned clothing for a numerous and lavish
household, some bolts of linen and woolen
cloth had been discovered, and a store of
knitting-yarns.

Betty was in black for David. All her

bright color was gone. Something of youth had left her, never to return, but there was in her grave and gentle look the quiet fortitude and decision with which frail and timid women often meet disaster and stand erect under crushing burdens. She did not speak of her bereavement at once, but of busy days. She had been of use to these poor, distracted women who had never had much to work with. Then she spoke of the happy children, who had forgotten that time of suffering and terror, and were having an unforgetable holiday in the freedom and joy of the woods of Isle le Beau.

Small fires were being replenished to cook the noonday meal, and Old Guard was rounding up the scattered children who were foraging with the squirrels for the falling nuts, when Johnny and Betty walked down to the tapering point of the island. Autumn rains had not yet begun, and the River Beautiful was at its lowest and clearest, a gently flowing current of heavenly blue. In the absence of shipping it had slipped back at once into its old, wild solitude.

Betty sat on a rocky grotto, so pale and still, with her chin cupped in her palm, that

Johnny's heart went out to her in that early passion of protecting love. He knew now that he must love her forever.

"Tired, Betty?"

"No. Thinking of all I must do—alone."

"It will come right. You will go to Marietta soon?"

"For the winter—until the war is over." She turned to him a face of bright bravery and high resolve. "We are going back. David would not rest in his soldier's grave with his children growing up in dependence. I will let his people help me with seed and tools and cattle; and that first family you rescued on the Scioto trail will go with us— strong young Germans who lost their all. I have too much land, and can make it worth while for them to stay with us for ten years. We can live in a half-faced camp the first year. It will be hard, but indeed, Johnny, I could not live anywhere else. The place is peopled with memories. There is a little, lonely grave. It will be long before we have such comforts, and our home will never be as beautiful again, but—"

"It shall be as beautiful. I am going back now."

She gave a little cry of fright and grief. Then her face kindled. "It—it makes one brave just to look at you. People tell me it will be so hard that it may well shorten my life."

Whatever his own sense of coming sorrow and loss, he could not but choose the best for her. "He who loseth his life shall find it."

"I never understood that before—why you have to go back now, and perish if you must." After she had eased her heart in quiet weeping, she spoke again. "There are so many things David wanted to do—give land for a school-house, have regular church services, clear the forest of wolves and breed sheep, send the boys to the academy at Marietta; do all the things that are necessary to keep the next generation around us from falling back into rudeness, ignorance and impiety. He left those tasks in trust to me."

As they walked back to the camp she told him that she would have some things of the old days to keep memory green. A week before the alarm she had had an impulse to gather up treasures of the heart—David's Bible, Johnny's little rocking-chair in which she had nursed all her children, Aunt Mary

Lake's cooky-jar, and her wedding-gown for
Mary's great day of happiness, and hide
them in the cave in the nursery. And now
she had another—Mrs. Blennerhasset's riding-
habit of scarlet broadcloth which had been
left in the workroom closet for repairs.

"I can see that kind and beautiful lady
every time I look at it—the Fairy Queen who
had only to wave her wand to give every
one pleasure. Out of that I shall make a cir-
cular cloak. The color of it in our soberly
clad lives! As a child I remember thinking
that no hour could be so dark and cold that
this glowing thing would not warm and
cheer it."

Nearly twenty years afterward, in an hour
of darkness, of bitter cold and wild storm,
Johnny remembered these wistful words and
spread that mantle above her. Now, with the
old look of pale exaltation, he parted from her
until the war should be ended, and crossed
to Belpré. He spent the short afternoon in
preparations for departure, made a supper of
apples, and camped in the cedar-grove on the
bluff.

Joy came with the morning that was crisp
with a light rime of hoar-frost. So early

that no one was stirring in the town, he rode through the fragrant orchards and out over the Bloody Way, to begin another dozen years of work that should make that ravaged wilderness bloom again.

X

FRESH FIELDS

A DOZEN years after the close of the war Johnny's new orchards blossomed and fruited in little towns and on well-cleared farms all the way out to the headwaters of the Miami, but Johnny was not there to see them.

For the thousands of people who had come to live in the Ohio River Valley the year eighteen hundred and twenty-five was marked by the completion of the Cumberland Road to Wheeling, Virginia, and by the journey to the new West of the Marquis de Lafayette. It was a triumph of pioneer energy and faith that the nation's aged guest was able to travel by post from the Potomac, and then by a palatial steamboat to St. Louis. Banquets and balls were given him in river ports of astonishing size and resources, and far up in Indiana, at the head of navigation on the Wabash, a venturesome settlement was made in that year and named in his honor.

It was thus that the floods of population and trade had fallen down the Ohio and backed up the larger tributaries. But behind and above these navigable streams the country of Johnny's beautiful labors was still heavily wooded and thinly settled, and must remain so until canals and railroads ended their isolation.

Even there, however, people were living in comfort and security. What Indians were left were confined to reservations; wild animals were disappearing, and little flocks fed on a thousand hills. Few children were more than five miles from a log school-house, and few families farther than a half-day's journey from a mill town near which Johnny had a flourishing nursery. In the matter of orchards this region, too, could now grow its own supply while the sower was off to fields unsown.

To the people of America a new door of dreams had been set ajar. With the booming of successive cannon from Buffalo to the Battery, an all-water route was opened through the Erie Canal, from the mountain-walled seaboard to the prairies and forests that lay back of Toledo and Detroit. Sailing-vessels and steamers from the old Indian trading-posts around the Great Lakes waited at the Niagara docks to transfer their wild cargoes of peltries, maple sugar, tan-bark, potash, dried huckleberries and boiled honey, to canal barges. They returned loaded to the guard-rails with eager emigrants and all their worldly goods. From the boat-yards of Cleveland, and from the orchards and corn-fields of the lake shore westward to Sandusky, Johnny had glimpses of the magnitude of this new migration as he went over his territory planting seeds, distributing trees, selling his nurseries to responsible men for the small sums that would outfit him for this new venture, and taking leave of old friends.

No one tried to dissuade him; indeed, many rejoiced. The setting sun has always been the shining goal of men, and America is still breeding a tribe of Israelites who move on, seeking the land of Canaan. Scarred veterans of pioneering in the rough hills of Ohio and western Pennsylvania also struck out for the level lands of Michigan and Indiana.

And no reason could be urged against his going. At fifty-one Johnny was ageless. His dark hair was pointed with silver, it is true, but his senses were as keen and his wiry figure as active, erect and tireless as they had ever been. To him time was an illusion of the mind, and seasons existed only in the soul. It was the springtime of life so long as the vision beckoned and the spirit leaped to some task undone.

He was now gleaning seeds at the cidermills in his earliest orchards at Chillicothe, Belpré and up the Muskingum Valley. Late in February he crossed from Zanesville to Columbus on short relays of horses that could be returned at once to their owners. On his way to Detroit he stopped for his farewell visit with Betty.

What changes the years had brought to the home on the old border which he had restored to beauty and she had kept together so bravely! At twenty the twin boys were in trade in Cincinnati, and, by much self-denial, paying Jimmy's way through Andover. In her seventeenth year Mary-go-'round had had a gay winter in Marietta. There she had lost her heart to Ethan Hildreth. He was a distant cousin of the literary physician who had long shared and then succeeded to the medical practice of the lamented Dr. True, and who indulged a harmless fad for keeping records of the weather. The gilded cock on the gable of Dr. Hildreth's house, that waved its tail feathers gallantly in the teeth of every wind, was the never-failing subject of facetious comment. When gibed about the restless habits of the bird, the doctor was wont to remark, dryly:

"You keep your ears open and you'll hear that rooster crow one of these days," and went off to add some item to the tabulated report which he made annually to the *American Journal of Science.*

Mary came home to wear her mother's yellowing wedding-gown and veil under the blushing trees of the orchard. It was she and her shrewd and energetic young Yankee husband who remained on the big, prospering farm. And now two babies of a new generation had begun to tumble out of a larger cabin into every happy day. 'Round her small world of home and social duties, for the place was the center of neighborhood life, Mary moved briskly on endless errands, with a cheerful ease and efficiency that were delightful to look upon. She greeted Johnny with the old affection, and then left him to visit with her mother.

Betty sat in his low rocking-chair, knitting a tiny red stocking, and with Mary's crowing baby on her lap. At forty there was not a white hair in her bright crown, but her large, wistful blue eyes seemed lost in her pale, delicately featured face. Mary, always tenderly conscious of her mother, turned a warning look on Johnny when he told his purpose, for Betty went still whiter and put her hand to her heart as if in a spasm of pain.

"Oh, Johnny! going so far away from us all, for so long a time?"

When he could he followed Mary out of doors. Fitful sunshine now and then broke through clouds, making the bare trees of the orchard etch their blue shadows on the snow.

"Isn't Betty well?"

"Who? Oh, mother! No one calls her that any more but you, Johnny. I thought you meant that fat rogue, Little Betty. Yes, I guess she's as well as usual. Anything startling always—" Her lips trembled. "I'll tell you just how it is, Johnny. In that terrible war-time her heart was injured. We children never knew until Jimmy went away to college last fall. Then, when there was no one to lean on her any more she gave way all at once. She might live for years, in much comfort, if she would only spare herself. She's the mind and heart and conscience of the country-side. Every one runs to her and wears her out. Watch her to-day and you'll see what I mean."

Ah, he did watch her with a proud and breaking heart. How lavishly she burned the oil of life to keep the light shining for less-endowed people who were stumbling up-ward along dim, rough ways. The old trail had become a main-traveled road, and all day passers-by dropped in to consult her—about raising money to keep the school going until corn-planting time; to cut the first pink calico dress a pretty, excited girl had ever owned, and to ask her to persuade the un-progressive not to oppose a much-needed road tax. She prevailed with the leader of the young men to give up the rude and cruel sport of a shooting-match. Then a new set-tler, of whom she had never heard before, came to say that the baby had died and his wife was distracted because no traveling preacher could be found for the funeral. Betty would go herself.

"Give the poor mother my loving sympathy and tell her that I'll come to say a few words, and fetch the singing-school so there will be music."

"There!" cried Mary, with helpless tears, when the comforted man was gone. "It's seven miles, Johnny, and such roads and weather! It will send her to bed for a week."

"Don't be so troubled about me—please, dear. I must go. A little bit of a baby cannot be put away in the cold earth without people being reminded that of such is the Kingdom of God."

When Mary was in the spare room, tacking a new quilt in the frame for a quilting-bee, Betty and Johnny had an hour alone; and because this might be a last parting they touched upon memories never spoken of before or afterward.

"Johnny, do you remember the night David brought me here, a bride? You—you lit the fire to welcome us home; and then we were sheltered with loving companionship, and you were out alone in the roofless night?"

"I would have stayed, Betty, if I could have borne it." Across the chasm of a quarter of a century of silence he looked his confession of a love foregone.

"I know," she murmured. "I think I have always known since the night Aunt Mary Lake died. There was no one in the world, then, as near and dear as you. If you—"

For the remaining years of his life he had the knowledge to bear that, if he could have chosen differently, her days on earth might have been longer. A glowing stick broke into coals and faded to an ashen rose on the hearth, and the clock on the chimney-shelf ticked away a little space of eternity. And then a look of brooding tenderness.

"You have not been unhappy, Johnny?"

"No, dear. My mission has filled the cup of life, and having you in the same world has made it overflow."

After another silence she laid her hand on his in gentle pressure. "You have made my life infinitely happier. I cannot imagine any world, here or hereafter, where you were not."

In the evening he stored up other memories

for years of solitary wandering. As the day darkened to a close the wind grew to a gale which penetrated the crevices of the house, so that Mary settled her mother in a high-backed chair and folded the scarlet cloak about her. The first new-born lamb of the season was brought in by the fire, and stories were told of brave and faithful Old Guard, who had run his race. With the two children in rosy sleep, Betty sitting with closed eyes and folded hands, Mary knitting, and Ethan Hildreth shaping a hickory ax-handle "to the fit of his own fists" with an almost pious absorption, Johnny rested his elbows on the hearth and read aloud by the light of the fire.

In a voice of extraordinary beauty, now loud and clear, now soft and thrilling, he amplified such texts as "Heaven is not outside a man, but within." Then with poetic imagery he pictured the Garden of God where every order of creation dwelt in harmony, and each found its own highest happiness and usefulness. Until the fire was covered for the night he lay marking guide - post passages to his hereafter in the copy of Swedenborg that he had bought for Betty. She was asleep when he departed in the morning, and, although he might never see her again, he would not have her awakened. But that night, unable to bear the comfort of any fireside where she was not, he lay out on a bleak hilltop, and to a cloud-wracked sky where no star glimmered lifted up his heart in prayer for her sweet, fading life.

By ways still wild from infrequent travel Johnny went up to a point on the Sandusky River where the Senecas had a small reservation. There he got an Indian guide and the loan of a horse through the bottomless, timbered morass of the Black Swamp to the rapids of the Maumee. To his dismay, he found the wide river that floundered in a trough of the low plain in raging flood, the waters thundering down the falls with the foam-crests of ocean surges.

His seeds were rafted across with difficulty, and he could do no planting in the saturated ground of the busy mill and transport towns which flanked the foot of the rapids. Nor could he get through the hundred miles of densely wooded and boggy bottoms to Fort Wayne. But he promised to come downstream with the flatboat - loads of wheat, corn and hogs in the autumn. Determined and optimistic people here were clearing and draining their rich lands, and had begun work on canals to the Miami and Wabash. When these should be completed—and Johnny's hundred-mile panorama of orchards in this valley had blossomed and fruited before that labor of Hercules was done—people would pour into an unhealthy region which had fewer settlers than before the war. Then the little log lake port of Toledo, that now stood up to its ears in mud and malaria, would rival Detroit.

Room was found for his two leather bags of seeds in a train of freight-wagons carrying flour, meal and pork to feed the transients who were passing through the old wilderness capital on the strait. Miles of grassy marshes and cranberry bogs, a dozen foaming streams with crumbling banks, sunken and tilted corduroy, and sloughs that would have floated boats, extended all the way up to the plank sidewalks of Detroit. Johnny paid his passage, at that time and for many seasons thereafter, by helping pry out mired wagons, get discouraged oxen on their legs again, and repair broken wagons at improvised forges.

JOHNNY APPLESEED

Even then the old gateway of armies and trade was a trim little city of white wooden houses and picket-fenced gardens. Standing in level green fields flanked by farms, with cattle grazing under trees that trailed their low branches in tranquil waters, and with every sort of craft anchored in the roadstead, it reminded a famous traveler, a decade later, of the quiet beauties of Holland.

As this was the season when most of the wild merchandise was brought in from the woods, the open spaces of the town were full of traders from distant posts; French trappers with their violins and their gaudily decked Indian wives; priests baptizing infants and giving in marriage; impish half-breeds, and majestic braves in beaver-skin blankets. These mingled in the streets and shops with elegant ladies of an old French and British aristocracy, with wealthy business men and government officials. And to this sufficiently strange and varied crowd was added the Yankees, New-Yorkers, planters from the Southern seaboard, Western pioneers, and the German, Dutch and Irish peasants, who poured up from a steamboat to gaze on the cliff-like forest wall through which they must break to reach their land of promise.

A day was required for goods to be tumbled out of the hold, for wagons to be loaded, and animals to find their land legs again. In a store crowded with time-pressed customers, where anything was to be had from a piano to a tomahawk, Johnny bought a suit of buckskin, cowhide boots water-proofed with deer tallow, a package of salt, and a bag of meal. For a stout pony he gave the last of his money to a mournful Ottawa. Loading his baggage on the animal, he was waiting in the Grand Circus for the forest-bound procession to form when a heavy hand clapped him on the shoulder.

"Good omen! I never thought to see Johnny Appleseed moon rise on the woods of Michigan." It was the Territorial Governor, Lewis Cass, who grasped his hand. "Were you going through Detroit without coming to see me?"

Johnny smiled. "There was no need. You have an orchard."

"True; and I also have a table and a fair library where I like to see the face of a brave man and a friend. Detroit has had its orchards, and its good living from Montreal, since early French days. But the country behind it is wilder than was Ohio when you and I came out to the Muskingum, with many more Indians and ravening beasts. However, we will be shipping flour to Buffalo in five years."

"No doubt of it," Johnny agreed.

"Well, dear pilgrim, I've cut a few roads for you to travel. Would a letter from me be of use to you?"

Johnny considered a moment. "No, I think not. One doesn't need a ticket of admission to men's hearts."

"You don't." The Governor compressed his lips and nodded in assent. Lifting his beaver hat with marked respect, he passed on.

With such a thrill as he had not felt since that eventful day in Pittsburg twenty-seven years before, Johnny went out on this heroic human tide. Men on saddle-horses led the way across the marshy ground to the west and into the woods. Families followed in democrat wagons with strings of laden animals, in carts, in frail chaises whose broken skeletons were left to bleach along this wild way,

and in the slow but sure ox-drawn prairie-
schooners. Those afoot, like Johnny, had
no trouble about keeping up, for in this
lacustrine land of ponds, wet depressions and
water-filled gullies there were no hills to
climb, and the stumps and fallen trees that
littered the ax-widened Sauk trail made all
travel slow. Ten years later, when this
forest-girt highway had become the post-road
to Chicago, it was still an obstructed mire,
with many unbridged streams.

But within a twelvemonth after the opening of the Erie Canal emigrants were pouring
over it eight months of the year. Every
mile of it out to the crossing of the St. Joseph
rang with axes, and every considerable stream
soon had a sawmill. No one could journey
over it for an hour without seeing smoke
curling up through the noble beeches and
ship-mast conifers. The narrower ravines
were spanned by tree trunks, and Johnny's
Indian pony "toed" these slippery foot-
bridges as easily as he; and at the sprawling
log tavern which marked the limit of a day's
travel, there was either a good ford or a tim-
ber-raft ferry worked with ropes and pulleys.

In a beautiful wilderness where friends

sprang up with the myriad delicate flowers of the forest, Johnny lived a second youth of eager joy in his mission. It was dangerous for a man to camp alone where huge bears, timber-wolves, lynxes, panthers and wildcats were so numerous and bold; but Johnny was seldom obliged to do that, for wayfarers were nearly always on the road. Or he managed to reach some lichened, beechwood cabin, where he slept on a pole-bed laced with rawhide, heaped with pine boughs and spread with deerskins. But except for his bag of meal he must often have gone hungry, for new-comers were living chiefly on game, and paying for their limitless acres with peltries.

Besides the problem of food, Johnny was perplexed to know where to put in his seeds. There were no hills or bluffs, and he was obliged to rail off corners of clearings or to fence in inclosures against barns or mills with slabs or brush. So he proceeded through the timbered plains, and through the "oak openings" farther west, where every cabin was raised in a grassy copse encircled by great trees. That was a gently rolling country of park-like beauty — of wide-spreading oaks, little hills and dancing brooks, and of sunny spaces sown with blossoms, where a gay woodpecker drummed on every ancient bole and the wood-thrush filled the bright, cool days with melody.

It was on an evening late in April, when his orchards in Ohio were in bloom and his heart ached for his old day in Paradise with Betty, that he reached the point on the St. Joseph where there was a crossing to the country of the Pottawatomies. Not for ten years was a white settlement made on the north bank, from which he now saw the camp-fire and skin lodges of a village of this numerous tribe that held the lands around the head of Lake Michigan. Following a couple of mounted braves who forded the broad stream by the light of pine-knot torches, he rode up the steep, wooded slope and sought shelter in a cabin that he was surprised to find on the edge of the Indian town. Pulling the latch-string, after the custom of the country, he walked in. A white woman, petticoated in deerskins like a squaw, screamed, and her rough husband dropped a shotgun.

"Thought it was them pesky redskins, stranger. Air you that appleseed mission-er?" Johnny's fame ran everywhere before him. "Haul up a stool and pitch into the grub."

But Johnny stood aloof in the doorway. "The Indians are peaceable. Why should they molest you?"

"Because I'm squattin' on their land, an' they're tryin' to scare me out. I'm willin' to pay, but—"

"You are not. You do not expect to pay, for you are well aware that they will not sell. You are a thief, and the meanest kind of an enemy of every decent white man in the country. If your family is killed the crime will be on your own head. I'll report your wicked trespassing to Governor Cass. When you move across the river I'll plant an orchard for you."

Sick at heart to find the old wrongs and hostilities springing up like poisonous weeds on this new border, he led his pony to the Indian village. That he had been Logan's brother would not commend him to a tribe that boasted the massacre of Fort Dearborn. But they had seen him leave the cabin a moment after entering, and the most unfriendly savage was disarmed by a claim on his hospitality.

"THOUGHT IT WAS THEM PESKY REDSKINS, STRANGER.
AIR YOU THAT APPLESEED MISSIONER?"

"I need food," he said, simply. "All men, white and red, are my brothers; but I do not break bread with thieves and trouble-makers. But leave that man alone. I will rid you of him without violence."

They made room for him at the fire. In the morning they offered to keep his tired pony on the fresh pasture, and to lend him a canoe to go down the historic "St. Joe" to Lake Michigan. There were already many cabins along the north bank of this stream that was navigable by steamboats. Near them he found sheltered nooks for his seeds in high banks; and he found coves back of the cliffs that sprang from the silver beach below the old French trading-post at the harbor mouth. In these northern lands the season was later than in Ohio, so, until the end of May, he continued his planting in a region where later generations reaped a millionfold. Long after his labor of love had ceased Michigan became the commercial orchard of the Middle West.

The new clearings were bannered with corn, and all the glades were red with wild strawberries when he returned to the Indian village. The tribe had refused to care for a nursery, but Chief Pokagon hitched a horse and an ox to a flaming chariot and drove Johnny down to the Tippecanoe River. He had reason to be proud of the wagon that he had made for himself, after no known model, long before a white man's vehicle was seen in that country. The hay-rack bed was mounted on hickory axles, and the solid wheels, hewn and burned and scraped out of cross-sections of a white-oak tree, were painted a bright vermilion. Until the Pottawatomies signed away their ancestral lands and went west of the Mississippi, Johnny could always count upon a lift of fifty miles in this triumphal car. Throned on a high seat beside the chief, who wore his war bonnet of eagle feathers, they rumbled across the lake-dotted prairies of northern Indiana, with its great herds of deer and buffalo. After crossing the shallow head-waters of the Tippecanoe, he and his pony were set on the southward trail.

A true Indian path in prairie country, it followed every turn of the eastern bank and clung to the shadow of the trees. Sheltered alike from sun and storm, it had a broad ribbon of water and a double belt of woodland between it and prairie fires. On the one

hand were ancient camping-places, all the forest fruits and blossoms, and the rapture of
thrushes; and on the other an emerald sea
of wind-rippled grass, with its fleets of cloud
shadows, and the fluting of the meadow-lark.
And all the way down to where it poured its
tribute into the Wabash the Tippecanoe had
every witchery of prairie streams—flowery
meads, and marshes sky-woven with water-
fowl; long stretches of bottom-land wooded
with sycamores, maples and hawthorns, and
deep, winding ravines brimming with beauty,
where the water twisted and foamed for miles
over rocky rapids.

Starting from the busy little year-old river
port of Lafayette, Johnny spent the summer exploring the enchanting valley of the
Upper Wabash, searching out the settlers in
the bottoms, the mills on the creeks, and the
"neighborhoods" of from six to ten cabins
on adjoining quarter-sections of prairie. People who had been on the treeless areas five
years had wood-lots growing from black wal-
nuts and the seeds of locusts, and they had
hedges of hawthorn shrubs and osage orange-
trees, planted on ditched and sodded ridges
for wind and fire breaks.

In the shelter of a few such living fences on the Wea and Wildcat prairies, in the knot of hills that overlooked Lafayette, and on bluffs above high water, Johnny began to put in his seeds. It was late in September, when the whistle of the first steamboat of the season was a Gabriel's trump over a forty-mile radius of country. During a month of dry and windless weather he worked rapidly upstream. From the sources of the Wabash he had only to make a twenty-mile portage across the low undulations of the watershed to reach Fort Wayne and the valley of the Maumee.

The prairie-grass had grown six feet high and turned brown. With sharp nights it lost its embroidery of purple and gold ray-flowers. Long imprisoned in forests, Johnny fell under the spell of these spaces bare and grand, arched over by wide, sun-drenched or starry domes, where the winds blew free and the spirit fared forth to brave adventure. Often before seeking shelter for the night he climbed a tree to look out over the sunset-gilded billows, with their horizon lines of blazing autumn woodlands. Wild herds were drowned in that ocean of herbage; cabin roofs were awash; the canvas-covered schooners of new-comers, the wagon-loads of corn and wheat, and the droves of hogs and cattle going down to flatboats on the river, plowed through like ships at sea, with parted waters in their wake.

But it was a landscape of terror as well as of beauty, where the vigilance of men never ceased. A spark from a careless hunter's fire, borne on a high west wind, would sweep a sea of flame over a fifty-mile prairie in an hour, often overtaking fleeing herds of deer and buffalo. Around every "neighborhood" the farmers mowed and burned a wide strip of grass and plowed the land as a protection. Johnny was cautioned to sleep in a cabin when he could, and to camp on the eastern banks of waterways, where he would find old Indian cobble-lined fire-holes in cleared spaces in the timber belts.

In the last week of October he reached the house of one of the few Scotchmen in the country. The man had a plot in the shelter of the thorny hedge ready for him, and, in a cold wind that threatened to blow the shock of red hair from his head, sat on a sawbuck and talked as Johnny worked.

"I hae a braw coatie o' buffalo-hide to fend the cauld frae ye. It cost me nae mair than a chairge o' pooder an' shot, so there's nae occasion for gratitude. But an orchard here is like the grace o' God. It canna be had for siller."

"The best things in life are those that cannot be bought."

"Ay, ye gang aboot gien yer bonny trees wi'oot price." By and by he remarked that it was blowing up to rain or to drive one of the deil's ain fires. His look was one of anxious concern. "Man, ye'll bide the blawy nicht?"

Johnny thought not. The planting season was short, and no time was to be lost. With such a wind at his back he could easily make the ten miles to the portage by nightfall and be in Fort Wayne the next evening. Filling the pockets of the warm fur coat with corn-dodgers and the hickory-nuts that the children had patiently picked out for him, he took the river trail.

With the waning day the wind increased. The sun set in a bank of fiery rose, with a smoky pall above it; and after it disappeared no light lingered on the plain, for a wrack of gray storm-clouds hid the moon and stars. In the darkness Johnny could not see to cross a steeply walled and watered ravine, nor could he venture to build a fire in the dry leaves and underbrush of the narrow belt of woods that topped the west bank. Tethering the pony under the trees and supplying him with grass, he ate his own supper, and with his half-empty bag of seeds for a pillow lay down with a huge hollow log to windward.

What with the roar of the wind and crowding thoughts, it was long before he slept. In the settlement which had grown up around "Mad Anthony's" old fort and Indian agency, a big plot would be ready for him, and men who had brought in corn and marsh-hay would be waiting to take him all the way out to Shane's Prairie and Twenty-four-mile Creek. Brave women were there who never winced if a bear or a panther scrambled across the roof, but who cried in their sleep for the bowery homes they had left in the East. Ah, what a mission! Again, as in Ohio, it was to be his privilege to feed the multitude in these new wilds with comfort and beauty.

He decided that he would leave his pony on the farm of William Worth near the town, and go down the Maumee with the flatboats. From Toledo he could make a quick passage to Erie, paying his way by pushing cord-wood under the boiler of a steamboat. Thence he could cross to his old gleaning-field in the Allegheny Valley. In the spring he could work his way down the Ohio and up the Miami to Piqua. Thus he could save time and energy—but for the first year since he had known her he would not see Betty! All he could hope for was to have word from her when he came into Pittsburg in February. Turning upon his bag of seeds he buried his face in his arm, and when he was at peace again he slept like a child.

And then, what dreams of sound and light in the moment before awaking! Upon the fabric of the wind—the loud moaning, the surf-rush of long grasses, and the threshing of the bare tree-tops—were woven filaments of sighs, silken rustlings and aerial whispers. A glow as of the rising sun was suddenly a burst of glory, as if the Creator had just spoken; and upon that were etched the black web of the trees, little flying birds and shooting stars. It was a puff of hot smoke, a blinding glare, the howling of wolves, the thunder of hoofs and the frantic plunging of the pony that brought him to his feet.

He leaped to get his hat over the faithful animal's eyes, but with an awful scream the pony broke loose and shot into that flaming sea. Shaking his blazing coat from him, Johnny fell down the bank, pursued by fire to the water's edge. Then a cloud of sparks and a billow of smoke rolled over him, filling the ravine.

There he lay immersed, with the smell of scorched fur and flesh in his nostrils, and the struggles and cries of suffocating and drowning creatures in his ears. Very soon, however, it was so still that he could hear the shallow water chuckling over its stony bed. The smoke lifted slowly, but, once it had risen to the prairie level, was whirled away on the wind. After a long time he crept up the farther bank and, burned, drenched and blinded, lay in a gale which blew itself out in gusts that were laden with the ashes and cinders of dead fires.

When he had recovered from the shock he had to consider if this was the end—if he, like his pony and his seeds, lay on the fiery death-bed of the prairies. Then he was not dismayed. He would leave nothing behind him but the unfinished task, and from that

HE LEAPED TO GET HIS HAT OVER THE FAITHFUL
ANIMAL'S EYES

God called men every hour. And all that
he valued was laid up in heaven or would join
him there. Into his heart he gathered his
treasured memories and beliefs—had a vision
of the orchards that he had planted to gladden
the eyes of men and angels. He summoned
the image of Betty, and the kindred spirits
of those who had gone before—relived hours
of happy companionship with them and an-
ticipated eternity until, from the agony of
his burns and the torture of morning light
to his eyes, he sank into unconsciousness.

Afterward he remembered that the clearest
vision of all was of Logan, who knew the wild
ways of these old lands of the Miamis in the
dark. As on that night in the Shawnee village on the Scioto, he felt the young chief's
arm about him, heard his voice calling:
"Brother! Brother! Brother!" until he
struggled up again from some abyss into which
he had slipped. He got to his feet, bandaged
his eyes, and without hesitation took an unseen path. When asked afterward how he
made his way to Fort Wayne, he answered
with simple and reverent conviction:

"I was led."

Three days later he staggered out of prairie-

grass higher than his head, to hear the tinkle
of cow-bells, and the laughing chatter of the
school-children who were out on the hilly
banks south of the town gathering hazelnuts.
His hair was singed unevenly, and a strip of
buckskin from his shirt was bound across his
eyes. In his fire-blackened and water-shrunk-
en garments, with his arms flung wide for the
support of gathered sheaves of grass, he was
such a figure as a farmer might have set up
for a scarecrow in a corn-field. But from his
firm, sweet lips came the gentlest speech these
startled young people had ever heard.

"Are there little children here?"

"Yes, sir." It was Billy Worth, a tall
boy of twelve, who spoke. They all picked
up their Indian baskets and, running across
the fire-strip of plowed ground, crowded
around him with the divine compassion of
childhood. Those prairie-bred little folk understood his terrible plight, for the fire in
which he had so nearly perished had been
watched with alarm from Fort Wayne.

"Will you lead me to a doctor?" And he
told his name. They looked upon him with
wondering awe, for they had heard of him
and his beautiful mission, as who in that

region had not? And when he added that
he had lost his seeds, but would have a new
supply to plant for them in the spring, emotional Madeleine Bourie, the small daughter
of a French trader of the place, covered his
blistered hand with tears and kisses.

"Saint from heaven, have you lost your
eyes, too?"

"No, dear little one; I hope not. But I
cannot bear the light." And it seemed that,
after three days of famine and torturing
pains, he could no longer bear his own weight
on his feet. He was sinking to his knees
when Billy set sturdy shoulders under his
arm.

"You lean on me, Johnny. I'm strong.
Jean Bourie, you get on the other side o'
him."

The evening glow was on land and river,
and on the rude but busy trading-post around
the old fort, when the children brought
Johnny slowly in across the fields.

XI

THE WINTER OF THE DEEP SNOW

Y the time sturdy apple-trees as tall as himself were growing in flourishing young orchards all over his new field of labor, Johnny was faring farther. His eyes had received no permanent injury from the prairie fire, and he was still in his full vigor; but at fifty-five the best man has fewer years and diminishing powers before him. With the feeling, unknown to youth, that no time was to be lost, his heart yearned over wildernesses unsown.

Therefore, in June of 1830, his eager feet took the road which Governor Cass had cut through the woods to the Grand River country. In that region, and along the numerous sandy inlets from Lake Michigan that penetrated the pineries, he left seeds for fall planting with the missionary priests who had rustic chapels in every cluster of huts of French and Indian trappers. And there the conviction grew upon him that menacing influences were abroad.

To the sower weather is the one, large, ever-present fact of the universe. He puts in his seeds early or late as he is permitted by kind or inclement skies. Then, unable to hasten or delay the harvest by any industry or cleverness of his own, he waits for the increase with anxious eyes on the heavens. A drought or flood, an untimely frost or rain or burning sun, may bring the labor of a year to naught. So he comes to note and to interpret every change in the temperature, the direction and force of the wind, the formation of the clouds and, especially, any variation from the normal in the pageantry of the seasons. In his three decades of planting in wild places, Johnny had gained all the weather wisdom of the farmer. A poet and seer besides, he was sensitive to disturbances in nature's harmonies. And now, discord had crashed across the rhythmic measures of the year, threatening to make one of those historic periods to which men refer back in some such descriptive phrase as "the year of the big wind."

WINTER OF THE DEEP SNOW

Beginning with the spring equinox, storms such as had not been known in a half-century had strewn the Atlantic coast with wreckage and swept up the valley of the Mississippi with destructive violence. All over the country the months of planting were cold and wet. Midsummer was oppressively hot, even in these northern woods and waters, with such electric tempests as made old hunters uneasy. Then, late in August, a day of sinister aspect—of a haloed and spotted sun which gave off pale-blue and violet rays—ended in a night that was made memorable by the most brilliant aurora ever seen by that generation of woodsmen. The women lit fresh candles before the images of Mother Mary and spent the ominous hours in prayer. This was followed by six weeks of stormy weather, with nocturnal illuminations.

At Muskegon Johnny found a half-breed Frenchman, so old that his merry little face was a scrap of crinkled brown crêpe, who predicted a long, cold winter, with deep snow and good hunting only for "M'sieu Wolf." He had no theory concerning it; but about fifty years before, when, as a young man, he had been at Prairie du Chien on the upper

Mississippi—"Oui, M'sieu, Dog Prairie"—
sunspots, bright northern lights and a bleak
and early autumn had been the forerunners
of a terrible season. From Montreal to Kas-
kaskia and the Rocky Mountains game was
destroyed by wolves, and many trappers never
returned to their stations. It struck Johnny
as significant that the Eastern newspapers he
had seen in Detroit in the spring, and this un-
lettered child of nature in the heart of the
continent, should agree in harking back a half-
century for comparison with this year's extraordinary weather. When he reached Marietta in the winter he would ask Dr. Hildreth
about this.

No one else could remember so far back,
and at first scant attention was paid to the
ancient *coureur du bois*. But in the weeks
which should have been mild and clear a
gray, heaving lake, sodden woods and "red
battles in the sky" stopped the violin-playing
and dancing of light-hearted vagabonds, and
filled Johnny with a sense of impending calamity.

In deep anxiety about his young orchards,
he went down to the trading-post at St.
Joseph in a mackinaw boat with hunters

who were obliged to go for their winter out-fits. From there he sent word over the road to Detroit that, in a season which might be severe, men should mulch the roots and wrap the trunks of their tender little apple-trees with straw and bagging. He would take the same warning down the Maumee from Fort Wayne, and send it back along the Wabash and White River valleys.

Then, in the brief allotment of ten days of Indian summer, after which cold rains and sharp nights set in, he had a profound experience. When he reached the ford of the St. Joseph on a still, hazy evening, he found the river so swollen that he hailed the Indian village for help in making the crossing. Chief Pokagon answered him and launched a canoe; but he stopped in midstream when a voice of worship and of love ineffable, as of an angel come down from the choir invisible, poured a flood of liquid melody out of the forest. It was the hermit-thrush. Never seen, and seldom heard to sing in this southern limit of the pines, the Indians called it the spirit bird. White man and red were tranced until that hymn of unearthly purity and beauty had ascended to the skies.

In the hush which followed, a cherished memory of Betty recurred to Johnny with such vividness that he saw again the gay and tender child of the cove above the shipyard at Marietta. With light, flying footsteps that seemed not to touch the grassy floor, she sped across a copse that was faintly silvered with moonlight. Turning with a happy smile, she waved her hand to him before she vanished in a belt of woods.

As he stepped into the canoe the chief gazed upon him with reverence, for now he knew what it was in Johnny's face that had arrested him at first sight, and then held him. It was some resemblance to the tribal tradition of Père Marquette, whose few, saintly years in these wilds, more than a hundred and fifty years before, had never been forgotten by the Indians. The face of that sinless man, who had constant speech with angels, had been a pale flame like an altar candle which had been blessed. Johnny had that look now. Had the spirit bird brought him a message?

He thought so. And he had seen something beautiful, reassuring him as to the well-being and happiness of a dear friend who had long been in failing health; but he could not fathom its meaning. He lay long that night thinking of the voice and the vision, and when the sky cleared and countless stars bloomed on the dark, he wondered if there were not one more softly shining for a soul returned to its home on the wings of that celestial song.

The next six weeks of the bleak weather, in which there was now and then an illuminated night, he spent among the settlements on the Maumee. From Toledo he worked his way on a Lake Erie steamboat to Cleveland. Journeying southward, he gleaned seeds along the Cuyahoga and Muskingum. It was his intention to go down the Ohio and up the Scioto, and to ease his aching loneliness by seeing Betty in March.

He was in Zanesville early in December, when his apprehensions were confirmed by another day of a dark-cratered sun, followed by an auroral display which kept awe-struck people out of doors all night.

The play of the northern lights began after sunset, in a blush that covered half the horizon. This mounted to a golden corona in the zenith, from which it presently fell in transparent drapery folds that wavered between pillars of crimson fire. Spindles of silvery luster darted from this, and through it the stars appeared as blue-white electric points. Stars innumerable glittered on a slate-colored southern sky. In a profound hush of nature the temperature dropped to an icy chill. The first large flakes of snow which wandered in the air at dawn were stained a lovely rose by the flickering light that lingered in the heavens.

Incredibly beautiful as was the spectacle, it aroused the superstitious fear of the ignorant and alarmed even the educated. Not within the memory of living men had such phenomena of the polar regions occurred in temperate latitudes. Now, Johnny learned, from New York and Boston newspapers, that the auroras he had seen in the wilds of Michigan were also reported from the Eastern seaboard and from the observatories of London and Paris. These singular occurrences, with their attendant storms, were not local. Whatever there was of menace in the air appeared to be enveloping the northern world. The succeeding days of wind and rain, snow and sleet and unseasonable cold filled every one with bewilderment and consternation.

WINTER OF THE DEEP SNOW

The Ohio Valley that was known to early pioneers had no such extremes of weather as are experienced in this semi-denuded region to-day. From the settlement at Marietta the winters had been uniformly mild. With grass until January, then light falls of snow that soon disappeared in soft thaws, and only an occasional "spell" of freezing temperatures, cattle were provided with little or no shelter. Corn was left in shocks in the fields and fuel in the woods, to be brought in as it was needed. Spring returned early in March, with blossoming trees and greening pastures.

But now the earth was saturated, then frozen, then swept by bitter winds and mantled with white. Over a road deserted by travel Johnny made his way southward, from one cider-mill to another, to find farmers putting up sheds for their cows and runners under their wagon-beds, as if this were New England. His own work was stopped by another storm in the week before Christmas. From heaps of pomace congealed to granite and buried under six inches of hard-packed snow, he could not wash out seeds. On the ice of the Muskingum he tramped down to Marietta.

Sleigh-bells were jingling merrily in a crisp day of cold sunshine, for every one who had a horse was out in a gay cutter or hastily contrived bobsled, to make the most of a winter sport that was usually of brief duration; and shouting children were snow-balling, coasting, and skating on Duck Creek. How it warmed the heart of any Yankee in exile—this typical New England town in the West! With its twin-towered "two-horn" church, its wide, tree-bordered streets, its colonial houses and prosperous little college, and now, with its ice-contracted flood and wooded hills all hoary with snow, it looked not unlike Burlington, Vermont. The last touch of similitude to a "down-east" port was given by the concern that was felt for an overdue steamboat from Pittsburg.

Johnny had other anxieties—the possibility that even his old orchards in Ohio might be winter-killed. Where long, severe seasons were the rule, apple-trees, like wise animals, grew thick, shaggy coats. But here, where even the delicate peach flourished, his trees had no such defense. Many of them kept, up to full maturity, the thin, satiny bark of rose canes. When he reached the town his canvas seed-bag was wet and frozen, so he hurried up to Dr. Hildreth's house and turned the precious contents out on sheets on the dry attic floor. Then he ran down to the front yard to find the weather-man.

Meteorology was then an experimental science and the subject of popular derision. For more than twenty years Dr. Hildreth had been, here, one of the dozen or so observers of the weather scattered over the eastern third of the country, who were without honor. A man of the slightest physique, muffled to his ears by an anxious wife, Johnny found him beside his little observation station, which looked like the shuttered belfry of a wooden church set up on posts on the lawn.

The gilded cock on the house gable was boxing the compass, in its laudable efforts to determine the direction of erratic gusts of wind. Seeing it so, a facetious neighbor hailed the doctor from the gate.

"If this is the kind of weather that 'tarnal rooster of yours brings, I'll wring his neck. I've got a cargo of pork and flour to ship to New Orleans, and the river is freezing over."

"Put runners under your old mud-scow and you can sledge it down over the ice pretty soon," was the doctor's advice.

The man went on, laughing, but Johnny asked, seriously: "Is that true?"

"I think it is, Johnny. A good many straws are blowing that way." He added, dryly, "I have quite a reputation as a humorist in this town, but if I am not much mistaken I am going to lose it this winter."

He opened the door of the airy little structure and, as eagerly as a boy to the interested listener, explained the various instruments within. And when Johnny told him about the recollections and predictions of the ancient, half-breed trapper in western Michigan, his hands shook with excitement and his thin, smooth-shaven, intellectual face glowed with the enthusiasm of the scientific investigator.

"Can he read? How old is he?"

"Not a word—no more than his pony. His speech is a rude, French-Indian patois in which nothing has been printed. He's eighty-five by the mission register."

"Such people often have wonderful memories—their minds are not cluttered up with thinking. This is interesting, undoubtedly reliable, for it confirms other data. Fifty-three years ago this winter your father and mine were at Valley Forge with Washington, trying to keep their discouraged souls in their freezing bodies. They, too, looked up at 'red battles in the sky,' and down at their bloody footprints in the deep snow of the severest season this country ever knew. Same signs this year—the atmosphere in an explosive state for months before, and winter setting in early and with unusual severity. In that winter of '77-'78 cattle, sheep and unlucky travelers perished everywhere north of Maryland, and many old orchards—"

He stopped at Johnny's stricken look, and made haste to put the matter in a more cheerful light.

"A surprising number of orchards did survive. It's truly wonderful how plants and animals adapt themselves. The wild geese and ducks fled southward this fall a month before their usual time, and my horse is growing a coat like a buffalo. The bark of the fruit-trees has roughened and thickened, and the buds squeezed up and fairly burrowed into the twigs. Men seem to have lost that protective instinct. The orchards will pull through all right, Johnny."

"They can be trusted to do their best." Johnny often startled people by speaking of his trees as though they were conscious beings. "But why do such seasons occur? What does it all mean?"

"Ah, that is what we are trying to find out! All we know is that once in two generations or so, varying from fifty to eighty years and coincident with sunspots and auroral displays, the magnetic conditions and cold of the polar regions descend to low latitudes. The periods vary in duration and intensity as in time. Let us hope that this explosion has spent itself."

Glancing at the instruments within before closing the door of the station, the doctor was shocked to see the rapidity with which the barometer was falling.

"Another storm coming, and that boat not in!"

The pale sun was still shining on the unsullied landscape when, in the face of amused merry - makers, the doctor unfurled a little black storm-flag from his gate-post.

"Ethan should be on that boat," he said

as they turned into the house. "He went to Boston in November for the sheep-breeders, to see if better prices could not be got for their wool. He was in Philadelphia last week, on his way home."

The streets of the town were suddenly emptied by a new snow-storm, which blew in on a thirty-mile gale at the darkening end of the day. A neighbor dropped in to ask what grudge the doctor had against the town that he should afflict it so. In the good old Puritan days in Salem he would have been burned for a wicked wizard.

After supper Johnny was sitting with the family before an open fire, where every one was too anxious about Ethan to talk or read, when the whistle of the steamboat was heard. A tortured thing, the thin, continuous shrieking was torn into shreds and whipped away on the roaring wind.

"I must go, my dear," the doctor insisted, as he and Johnny slipped into overcoats. "There will be sick and possibly injured people on that boat. Have a hot supper and a warm bed ready for Ethan. I may be delayed, but Johnny can fetch him up."

Only in the larger cities were streets lighted

in that day, but curtains were drawn back and the glow of fires and whale-oil lamps flared into the storm. The scared faces of women and children could be seen pressed to window-panes. From every house men ran out and down Muskingum Street to the wharf.

The wind, racing counter to the current, had heaped up the water in the narrowed channel until it was a welter of foam-crested billows and wallowing troughs. The boat could not be seen, but its shrill whistling, straining labor, and slithering crashes through shore ice could be heard above all the noises of wind and flood. Like a specter it loomed out of flying clouds of snow, keeled over and smashed into the slip.

A cheer went up. As soon as the gang-plank was run out Johnny went aboard with other men to carry fainting, hysterical and battered passengers off and into the shelter of the nearest warehouse. The crowd had begun to disperse when he ran to the doctor.

"Ethan didn't come!"

"Are you sure?"

"Yes. The captain said there had been heavy snowfalls on the mountains and the stage-coach had not got in when he left. No mail from the East for a week."

The doctor collapsed on a bale of wool, white as a tallow candle. "This is serious! No telling when another boat can get through. If the temperature continues to fall the river will soon freeze over. Johnny, Mary is up there on the farm, with no help besides a bound boy of sixteen, and she has a frail young baby. Ethan brought in enough fuel for an ordinary winter before he left, but not enough for such a season as this. That hollow of the hills is a perfect trap for snow. This little family of my own blood may be snowed under and frozen to death."

And Mary had a frail mother to care for, too! Johnny's heart leaped to Betty in this new peril, but he did not speak of her. Except to Mary, he never spoke Betty's name. In a sacred reticence he had always held her locked in the inner shrine. Now he said, simply:

"Don't worry about that. It will be all right. I am going up there. When Ethan can get through have him fetch my seeds."

"You can't do it, Johnny! It's a hundred and fifty miles. You might make the rest of the way if you could get a boat to Chilli-cothe. No horse could travel such a distance in this weather."

"I wouldn't think of taking a horse. If Ethan had come on this boat he would have gone on?"

"Oh yes, certainly; he would probably have perished, but no consideration could have held him, with his family in such a plight."

"Nothing can hold me." Johnny's eyes burned, and his colorless face was drawn with emotional strain. There was some mystery here—some old grief that had never lost its keen edge of pain. The doctor had always known that a special tie bound Johnny to Mary's family, but into the nature of it this gentleman of delicate mind had no desire to pry. But he felt the passionate strength of it in the quiet voice and restrained speech: "Any man can do what he must."

"At least you will wait until this storm is over?"

"I will not wait a moment after daylight. It may storm all winter. You think so your-self. I will go down-shore through Belpré to Hockingport, and up the Hocking River over the ice. There are villages and farms all along the way, and no hills to climb. I can make it in ten days, even if there are drifts and with the wind in my face."

Johnny was asleep in ten minutes after he reached the house, renewing his powers for the ordeal before him. But no other one of that prayerful household slept soundly through the hours in which the wind moaned in the chimneys, tormented the trees and shook the sashes. By lamplight the next morning he was trussed in woolen clothing and furs and provided like an Arctic explorer. The doctor added blue goggles to protect his eyes from snow-blindness. Word of his intention had filtered through the storm-bound town, and a dozen hero-worshiping boys appeared to pilot him across the Muskingum and to cheer him lustily from the site of old Fort Harmer. His answering halloos were borne back to them after he was lost to view in the snow-veiled woods.

Sleet had fallen in the night and formed a crust as smooth as glass, but not strong enough to bear his weight. Through this he broke at every step. The temperature had dropped to five degrees below zero, and it was snowing, again, in stinging pellets as fine and

hard as sand, driven by a furious gale. There
would have been some shelter in the forest,
but the road had disappeared, and he dared
not risk losing his way. Facing the full force
of the wind, he made his way from tree to
tree along the edge of the woods. Now and
then he had a glimpse of the narrowing strip
of gray water. Every hour or so he stopped
at a farm-house to get warm and to drink
black coffee. In Belpré, where he slept, he
got flat staves at the cooper-shop and fitted
them with leather straps. On these ski-like
snow-shoes, in a lull of the storm, he sped
over the shore ice to Hockingport.

He could not use these helps in the valley
of the Hocking, where loose snow had been
blown down from the hills and heaped in
drifts. Then the sky opened again, and a
cataract of fleece as soft and thick as wool
tumbled down and was broken to foam
on a river of wind. Against this blast he
struggled along the low growth of the bank,
passing a town and a number of farms un-
wittingly. Once, the near-by house obliterated, he stood among cattle huddled in the lee
of a stable. A haystack looming out of the
smother, he burrowed into it to sleep.

ON THESE SKI-LIKE SNOW-SHOES HE SPED OVER
THE SHORE ICE

JOHNNY APPLESEED

Not until late in the spring did the people of Ohio learn that the entire Mississippi Valley was in the grip of this storm, which opened with a crash in the last week of December. A wonder, at first, it soon became a terror, then a benumbing, bewildering horror, as it raged for days unabated. Changing in character from time to time—running the gamut of rain and snow and sleet, veering winds and minus zero temperatures—it continued to imperil the lives of men and animals. Travelers caught out in it lay over for days in the first shelter to be found. In a few historic instances men did get through; but many more perished. When the snow went off in March the bodies of strangers were found in the woods and on the prairies. And this was but the overture to a winter of storm.

Johnny went on. The only sign of life, now, in storm-beleaguered villages, was the faint glimmer of light through snow-incrusted windows. In spite of huge fires, farm-houses were cold. Shelterless cattle were turned into fields to help themselves to what food they could paw and pull from shocks and stacks. With creeks, ponds and wells frozen, men were melting snow in soap-kettles which were fitted into the tops of brick and clay ovens under sheds in the yards. Ropes were stretched from doors to barns and to buried wood-piles, to guide men in and out on life-saving errands.

At the end of ten days he had reached the upper end of the Hocking Valley, and was obliged to skirt the hills and to make his way across a tract of tangled marshland to the Scioto. For miles here there were no houses. All landmarks had disappeared. Once a wolf tracked him for a long distance, for there were still a few of these raiders of the flocks in the rough hills of Ohio. His feet were frost-bitten when he reached the river-bank and was guided to a house by a glimmer of light through the gauzy veils of snow. There, unable to get his boots on, he was obliged to lie over for a day. The delay was an eternity of mental agony, for the situation of people had become alarming. Every family was marooned, with starving and freezing cattle and diminishing wood-piles.

By noon the next day he was able to speed up the river on his snow-shoes, over a new, glazed surface. But when he turned west-ward into the creek he faced a bitter wind and a dazzling light on the glittering ice, for against the gray sky a white sun shone for a time, its disk clearly marked by a halo of prismatic colors. A slaty dome was darkening above the white fields when he reached the home of his heart.

In that trap for drifting snow the house was sunk to the window-sills. But cheerful firelight glowed through the panes and from an out-oven under a shed. There, as he thought, the bound boy was shoveling snow into the big iron kettle. Hearing his footsteps crunching through the crust as he stumbled up into the yard, the figure turned. It was Mary, in a suit of Ethan's old working-clothes, who dropped the shovel and ran toward him.

"Ethan! Oh my dear, my dear! Thank God you have come!"

"It's Johnny, Mary!" He caught her and held her while she sobbed on his shoulder. "Why, Mary, dear little Mary-go-'round, this isn't like you! Ethan's all right. He missed the boat, so, of course, I came."

She laughed and wept hysterically. "I don't know which I've been the most afraid of—that Ethan would come, or that he wouldn't. So much trouble this year, all coming at once, has sapped my courage and strength. I guess there isn't—quite enough of me—to go 'round—this time, Johnny."

"Why are you doing such work as this? Where's that boy?"

"Otto? Getting the sheep into the fold that he boarded in on the hill-slope under the barn floor. He's a good, strong, German boy, Johnny, doing more than a man's work. We have to keep this fire going to supply the stock and the house with water."

"Well, go in now and see if you can cook enough for two men." He was extraordinarily happy as he took up a pail of water and followed her along the tunnel-like path to the house. His orchards were resisting the weather, and it was his blessed privilege to protect and cherish Betty and her loved ones until Ethan should return.

For an hour he melted snow, and worked about the animals which were crowded into the stable, whistling all the while. Then he milked the cows. Now for a heartening supper, ease for his frost-bitten feet, and an evening of joy! The wind had died down and sparkling stars come out when he started toward the house again. Then the hush, the icy chill, the rosy blush spreading along the horizon and climbing to the zenith in pulsing flares of splendor! In a stillness broken only by electric cracklings in the air, the snow-laden trees in the orchard were stained to a sardonic semblance of the April blossoming.

Another storm! No rest, now, no safety for any one, until, in frantic haste, more work was done. In such apprehension as he had never before felt, he went in and set the pails of milk on the floor. No one was in the low-ceiled, fire-lit living-room; no breath of wind was stirring, but, as he opened the door, Betty's little empty chair swayed lightly on its rockers. A surge of memory swept him back to the hour and the room in which Mary Lake had died. A wistful, hovering presence, loath to leave those long loved on earth, her spirit had seemed to linger before taking its final flight. This room, too, had its gentle ghost.

Hearing him, Mary hastened in from the kitchen. The face of the delicate baby on her arm was a snowdrop against her sable breast, for Mary was dressed in the unrelieved black of mourning. At that he cried out, hoarsely:

"Where's Betty?"

She burst into tears, her grief fresh at the sight of his.

"Oh, Johnny, I didn't know where to write, you move about so. Didn't Dr. Hildreth tell you? Mother—died—suddenly—three months ago."

XII

UNDYING LOVE

H E stood there, stunned by the shock, shaken to the foundations of his faith, that Betty could drop out of life and he live on, unknowing, and with no sense of loss. Then a comforting reassurance filled his mind and heart. He had known! And he had not lost her! When he spoke it was in assertion:

"It was early in October; in that brief season of Indian summer."

"Yes, Johnny, but you could not know!"

"I knew! She told me about it herself, but I did not understand." He described the heavenly voice with its tidings of great joy, preparing his soul for the vision of that hazy moonlit evening on the St. Joseph River. "She appeared to me like that to comfort us all with the thought that she was as well

284

and happy as the little girl I knew and loved
in Marietta—immortally young and well and
happy, all her cares and pains and tragic
memories fallen from her. Oh, Mary, heaven
is not far away, but within and close around
us." Then with entire unconsciousness he
used one of Betty's endearing mannerisms of
speech: "Don't cry so; please, dear. It
grieves her."

It gave her the strange, consoling feeling
that her mother was speaking to her through
him. As the chill of the dropping temperature penetrated the house and the pathetic,
uncomplaining child shivered in her arms,
she went to Betty's wardrobe-chest and took
out the scarlet cloak to wrap around it.

"I could not bear to use this before, Johnny, but now I can. Nothing else seems to
keep my pale little Blossom so warm." The
splendid color trailing to the floor, and Mary's
words, reminded him of Betty's girlish fancy
about Mrs. Blennerhasset's riding-habit: "No
day could be so dark and cold but that glowing thing would warm and cheer it."

Now he had something to say that would
try the soul of the bravest: "That is your
part, Mary, to stay in the house, cherish this

frail little life, and keep us all warm and in good cheer. Can you be brave? Another storm is coming; and Dr. Hildreth thinks it may storm all winter, as it did in that terrible season of Valley Forge. Ethan may not be able to get through until spring. Let us pray that he may not try."

She went white and swallowed hard, but with a new understanding of their peril, and gratitude for the love which had impelled him to make this desperate journey for their protection, she returned his look with one of resolute courage.

"I should be ashamed to fail you, Johnny. Tell me what I must do."

"Get supper at once," was his practical suggestion. "Otto and I will need plenty of hot food to keep us going for some hours yet."

In a moment, so did he imbue them all with his undismayed spirit, the household, which for two weeks had lived in a state of half-paralyzed alarm, began to wear its normal aspect of cheerful industry. While one child laid the table and Mary prepared supper, Little Betty sat in the low rocking-chair and held the baby. With two boisterous little ones scrambling over him, and a tired collie sprawling and lolling at his feet, Johnny took the strong and willing German boy into his confidence.

After a hasty meal they went out together, comrades in arms for the weeks of battling with arctic weather which lay before them. By the spectral illuminations in the sky they stretched guide-ropes to outbuildings, bedded the stock, fetched in a week's supply of wood, and, digging the rest of the fuel out of the snow, stored it in the oven-shed. It was ten o'clock when they came in, the boy to fall asleep at once in his warm feather-bed in the loft, and Johnny— His days of mental and physical strain, followed by the spiritual shock, and that by further hours of toil, had brought their reaction of mood. He stood within the door, struggling for self-control, hollow-eyed with the torturing fear that Betty might have been laid away in that most desolate and forlorn of all earthly places —the remote and neglected country burying-ground. He could not bear to think of her as forsaken, out alone in the cold and darkness and coming storm.

"Where—where is she, Mary?"

JOHNNY APPLESEED

"In the orchard, Johnny, under the tree with the drooping branches, where she loved to sit in the little rocking-chair."

He went out again to pace the drifted aisles, and to sit on the bench under the twin trees where, on one morning of many a spring, he had wakened to see her so blithe and happy under the tent of pink bloom. Now he watched beside her frozen bed, questioning his guidance. He had left her, and through danger, hardship and grief she had come to this untimely end. The snow laid so deep above her was spread with reflections from the cold fires in the sky, a mockery of the comfort and glow of the fireside; and the snow-burdened, rose-tinted trees of his generation of patient planting and yearning love might well have their next blooming beside the River of Life. Had his sacrifice been in vain?

Chilled to the bone, trembling with exhaustion, filled with profound spiritual confusion, for even the angels, he believed, have their hours of dark discouragement and separation from God, he returned to the house. On the hearth he passed his hand across his eyes in an effort to recall some urgent reality of the physical world.

"There is something—I think my feet need some attention, Mary."

They were white and shrunken with frost. When thawed out to a swollen and burning redness he was obliged to sit helpless for two days, while a fresh fall of snow was laid to the depth of fifteen more inches over the entire Mississippi Valley. But, in Ethan's larger socks and boots, he was out in the blizzard of wind which blew the loose snow down from the circling ridge.

No morning dawned thereafter in which the temperature was above zero. Day after gray, lowery day the wind was a steady, fierce gale with new snow falling, or old snow blowing before it. Fences, corn-shocks and low outbuildings were submerged. Doors banked overnight had to be cleared for exit, windows for daylight; runways plowed in the barn-yard so animals could be let out for air and exercise; snow broken up and shoveled from under orchard trees, when the lower limbs lay on the surface and bruised their bark by threshing over a glazing of sleet. And, daily, snow had to be melted for water; corn, hay and bedding-straw dug out of frozen tombs; feed cut up for sheep, and warmed for pigs and chickens.

The house was well stocked with food, but as the bitter weather continued unabated, and the supply of fuel ran low, all Johnny's waking hours and troubled dreams were filled with alarm. Ethan had left a quantity of cord-wood in the forest, but even if it could be located and uncovered horses could not be driven into the woods where low branches rested on the ground, and their legs could not plumb the great depths of crusted layers of snow. Johnny and Otto felled small trees along the creek, and dragged the logs up into the yard with ropes. This wood was wet and green, and warmed the house so ill that on the coldest days the children were kept in bed.

By incessant toil and sleepless vigilance the twin specters of freezing and famine were kept at bay; but the bitter cold, biting winds and bewildering blurs or stinging blasts of snow became an obsession. And there was danger to the mind in this storm-beleaguered isolation. From the last week of December no travelers were seen on the road. Rarely did the air clear sufficiently for the nearest neighbor, a half-mile distant, to be hailed with dinner-horn and fluttered table-cloth;

and if a letter from Ethan lay in the village post-office, three miles away, it might as well have been in the moon. Upon their hearts lay the unspoken fear that Ethan might have tried to get through, and was now lost in some tragic mystery never to be solved until Judgment Day. For all they knew, the earth had swung into some cataclysmic cycle and lay forever congealed, all life locked in crystal prisons, to be sepultured in immemorial snow.

The white mantle had lain unsullied on the frozen earth for ten weeks, and had increased to the depth of four feet on the level, with every valley, hollow, forest, fence and building a trap for deeper drifts, when Johnny was awakened one morning in March by the sound of water dripping from the eaves. He scrambled into his clothing and ran out into the soft glow of the rising sun and a balmy southern breeze.

"A thaw, Mary! The snow is going off!" he cried. He was wild with relief himself, and Mary broke into such tears and laughter as frightened the children when she gathered them into her arms for morning prayers.

It was true! It was unbelievably true that

water was dripping everywhere, from eaves
and trees, and trickling away in clear riv-
ulets. Avalanches slid from roofs; trees
dropped their white burdens; buried things
emerged, and the snow sank visibly. In three
days they watched the wild ducks and geese
go north, hour after hour, in hurrying flight.
Then the sky brightened; patches and fringes
of misty emerald appeared; song-sparrows,
phœbes and bluebirds arrived, and the buds
swelled and turned green on the lilac-bushes
and fruit-trees. The orchards had weath-
ered this historic winter!

With a bright apple-twig in his button-
hole, Johnny went slopping about in the
wet, making preparations for the coming
flood. Soon Betty would have her tender
coverlet of grass, and birds and blossoms
would burst into song, color and perfume
above her. He could bear to think of
her as here in this dear, familiar place, cherished by those she had loved. All summer
she would lie in shine and shade and shower,
under silver moon and soft starlight, and in
his beneficent wanderings he would have
her with him, in spirit, under the same
kind canopy.

And now he could bear another thing which had haunted his nights of sleepless pain. It was certain that, in the Northern woods and on the treeless prairies, the snow must have lain deeper, the temperatures fallen lower, the wind raged with destructive force. Undoubtedly his nurseries and young orchards in Michigan and Indiana had perished, and his five years of labor there been brought to naught. But that was of small importance compared with the suffering, and the loss of crops and live-stock, by thousands of new settlers who would sink at once into deeper poverty. It was his to keep them from falling into despair. Better luck next time! Better days coming!

The vision of sublime service to humanity brightened and beckoned as the blossoming maples began to light their fires of spring along the edges of the woods and watercourses. He waited only on Ethan's return with his seeds to be off to his blighted fields.

Before the end of that week of thaw, the ice of the snow-flooded creek suddenly broke up and went out with the crashing reports of artillery. Water swept up the lawn to the door-step, and a wild torrent uprooted trees and carried them away, together with small buildings and luckless animals. In the stable at the time, Johnny ran out, driving the horses before him and shouting to Otto and the collie to get the cattle and sheep up on higher ground. Mary, standing in the doorway, screamed a warning as the oven-shed was whirled into the flood; but Johnny saw the danger too late. Struck by a corner of the roof, he went down.

The dog dragged him out, and Mary, struggling through rushing, ice-blocked water to her knees, led him to the house. Dazed by the blow, he still remembered his errand of mercy and would have broken from her, but she made him understand, at last, that the animals had all swum to safety. She bandaged the swelling bruise on his head; but when she had got him into bed he sank, almost at once, into a dreadful stupor with heavy, labored breathing.

No help for him who had kept them all from perishing! When he became violently ill, the utmost that she could do was to try to relieve his headache and nausea; and when fever came up and he wandered in his mind, she sat beside him in tearless anguish and kept cold water on his burning, restless head. She scarcely noticed the rapid going down of the flood, the sudden disappearance of the sun at midday, the slaty sky of night glittering with blue-white electric points, the flickering fires which played with sinister splendor along the northern horizon, or the icy chill of the air.

The last of the green wood was gone. Otto built up a smoking, sputtering fire with the water-soaked wreckage strewn about the yard. That night the soft earth and the creek, which had returned to its channel, were frozen to iron. Then on a polar gale the wild water-fowl fled southward from frigid lands of famine. The leaden sky of dawn was black with them, screaming before the blast. For two days the house rocked in the arctic tempest, and the world was obliterated in flying clouds of snow as thick and impenetrable as a fog at sea.

Through all the noises and horrors of that storm Johnny raved in delirium. At times it took both Mary and Otto to hold him in bed. He cried out for his seeds, and was comforted only for the moment by the assurance that Ethan would fetch them. When he reached out his arms for the little rocking-chair, Mary brought it to the bedside; and when he stared at the scarlet cloak hanging on the wall and muttered about the cold, she spread it over him. But when he begged her to put it over Betty to warm and cheer her, she knew nothing of that old memory which surged up and beat upon his heart, and could only weep in her helplessness.

"Oh, Johnny, try to remember! Mother is warm and happy in heaven."

As the storm died away in fitful gusts of sleet, and the cold hardened to minus degrees that chilled the blood, he became quieter. Thinking that he slept at last, and praying for Ethan to come in this extremity of peril, Mary lay down, without undressing, to nurse the baby whose delicate bloom of reviving life she owed to Johnny's care of them all.

Then her exhaustion betrayed her. In the blessed silence and darkness, after that long time of storm and stress, she fell asleep. The first things of which she was vaguely aware, in the early hours of morning, were the frantic barking of the dog, and the river of cold which was flowing through the house. And whether in her dream or waking she never knew, but she heard her mother's voice:

"Mary, you go 'round, dear, and look after Johnny."

How sweet it was—the gentle tones, the quaint phrase treasured in her memory. But this was not spoken in the old manner of reminding a thoughtless child of duty in the midst of play, but was anxious, insistent, pleading:

"Mary, Mary, Mary! You go 'round, dear, and look after Johnny!"

She suddenly sat up, wide awake and with a sense of danger. Somewhere in the yard the dog was barking continuously in wild alarm. The door was open. Johnny's bed was empty.

She found him, the collie standing guard beside him, lying cold and senseless on Betty's snowy grave, over which he had spread the warm, red cloak. When she and Otto had carried him in, Mary put the brooms, the butter-bowls, the children's stools—every small, dry, wooden thing at hand—into the fire to heat blankets and water, and bade the frightened boy strip the fences of their top rails.

"Keep the fire going! Burn every fence and building on the place, if you must, but keep up the fire! Here is one of God's angels perishing."

It was an hour before Johnny's heart beat with its full force, and from the death-like chill he passed into fever and delirium. The day dawned bright and still and intensely cold, the sun shining on dazzling fields of ice-glazed snow, and waking a million sparkles from swollen green buds frozen in the hearts of icicles.

They were all around his bed—Mary and Ethan, and the good doctor for whom Ethan had "swum through high water to Columbus," on the bleak April day that Johnny returned to consciousness. A winter that had streaked young Ethan's head with silver had bleached Johnny's hair and beard to the snowy whiteness of the pillow on which he lay. He knew them, and the old smile of love and gentle happiness lighted his cavernous eyes and wasted face; but in a moment he looked beyond them, around the room, in wistful inquiry. Mary had to lean over him to hear the faintly spoken words:

"Where's Betty?"

"Why, Johnny, don't you remember?"
And then, seeing how it was with him, that
he mercifully remembered nothing of the sorrow and terror and hardships of that nightmare of a winter, she finished, "Mother's
in the orchard, Johnny."

"Are the trees in bloom?"

"Not—not yet." The fruit-trees of Ohio
did grow another set of buds, and, late in
May, put forth a few, pale, scattered blooms.

His presence here, in this home of his heart,
seemed perfectly natural, and about his ill-
ness he expressed neither surprise nor curi-
osity, but accepted it with the unquestion-
ing simplicity and patience of a child. They
all hung upon his next words.

"Betty will want—her little rocking-chair."

Ethan jumped up. "That's right, Johnny. Don't you let me forget my manners."

He carried the chair out to the orchard.
Mary found him there on Johnny's bench,
his gaunt face buried in his hands. His
arms tightened around her and the precious
little rosy Blossom on her breast.

"Mary, while I lay in Marietta with the
broken rib I got in the boat-wreck, I should
have gone raving mad if I had not known

that Johnny was here. To think that I should find you all safe and well, not even a silly sheep lost, and him lying like that! And I dropped his seeds in the flood when the ice went out under me on the Scioto." He clenched his fists, and the few, slow, difficult tears of the man of Puritan ancestry were squeezed out and hung on his lashes. "I'd sweat blood to have Johnny his old self again and to get his seeds back for him."

"It is unlikely that he will ever ask for them," the doctor said, as he joined them. "He has had a concussion of the brain from the blow on his head, and that was followed by brain-fever of such severity and persistency that his recovery is surprising. Has he been under mental strain or suffered some emotional shock?"

Since the mischief was done and it would avail nothing, Mary could not speak of the effect of her mother's death on Johnny. "He felt responsible for all of us and worked far beyond his strength. And he was anxious about the orchards, especially his young trees and nurseries farther west—slept ill all winter," she said. As long as she lived she never could forget how often he had got up in the night to pace the floor of his little room for hours, or to go out to lonely vigils by Betty's ice-locked grave; and she could never speak of that time to any one but Ethan.

"It has been a trying season for every one," was the doctor's sober comment. "The minds of many people have been more or less affected. Johnny's young plantations in the West have all been destroyed, I am afraid, with the crops and stock and much of the game, for the snow lay ten feet deep on the prairies. He may always be spared the knowledge of this loss, for there is a lapse of memory extending over several years, and some mental confusion. Well, Ohio has its orchards—a debt to Johnny that we can never pay. It will be a long time before he gets back his physical vigor, but be patient and hopeful. I think he will improve in both body and mind. Just now" — he tapped his own head significantly—"Johnny isn't all here."

When he was gone Mary turned and wept on Ethan's breast. "Oh, my dear, my dear, I understand Johnny's devotion to us who never did anything to deserve it. Once in his ravings he cried out, 'I'll take care of your babies, Betty!' He rescued us all in the war, he made this home beautiful for us twice, and he always has watched over us. In some strange way that I am content never to know, he belonged to mother. Now he is ours, to love and hold in reverence, and, if he is always to be like this, to care for tenderly as long as he lives."

Ethan wrote at once to his cousin, Dr. Hildreth, to assure him that the family and stock had come through the winter unharmed, owing to Johnny's care, and that Johnny himself had been seriously ill, but was now recovering. As there would be no seed for his gleaning this year, people must not be alarmed if he was not seen along his old routes.

"Nothing keeps so well as bad news," he remarked to Mary as he sealed the letter. "Let us work and pray that in another year there will be none to tell about Johnny."

As a beginning in that labor of love Mary laid aside the mourning which bewildered and distressed him. By and by he ceased to ask for Betty. It was as though he had found her and was companioned by some presence, invisible to others, in which he had a quiet happiness. The little rocking-chair, with the scarlet cloak thrown over it, stood by his bedside, and when he got up it was returned to its old place on the hearth. Often when Johnny lay before the fire with his Bible or other book, he looked up at whoever might be sitting in it, smiled, and read something aloud. They soon learned that he loved to see it occupied by Mary or Little Betty, with the baby in arms.

Ethan cleared the yard of wreckage, cut away dead and broken limbs, and grubbed out winter-killed trees and shrubbery; and the children gathered up and buried the many little bundles of feathers which lay under perches. Everything possible was done to give the place its normal, seasonal aspect; but the summer which followed the winter of the deep snow was dark and inclement. They were anxious about the effect upon Johnny the first time he came out into a day of threatening clouds and fitful sunshine. Puzzled by the sodden, dropping leaves, the absence of bloom and fruit, and by the scarcity of birds and bees, he asked:

"What season is it?"

"It's June, Johnny."

"But there are no apples!"

"Ohio has been lucky, but we must expect a crop failure now and then." Ethan tried to speak lightly, but it was difficult not to be candid with Johnny. "A freeze in March killed the first buds, and the season has been bad for everything."

He stared at them wildly "I never heard of such a thing happening in Ohio. I—I don't remember anything about it."

"You were very ill at the time, Johnny." In spite of her the tears welled into Mary's eyes, his bewilderment and distress were so piteous. But she was inspired to add: "You know you always stop to spend a day with— with mother in the spring."

The mystery cleared, he lost his look of alarm, and, his interest in himself always of the slightest, he dismissed the matter from his mind. "Are the orchards like this all over Ohio?"

Ethan nodded, and they waited with suspended breath, half fearing, half hoping that he would ask for the seeds lost in the flood and for his blighted plantations in Michigan and Indiana. But for him those disasters had never happened and Betty had never died. As it was with her, all his cares and pains and tragic memories had fallen from him. He held only to the great fundamentals —his undying love for her and his beneficent purpose. "There will be no seeds this year," he said, but not sadly. His face took on the look it had worn in his youth in Pittsburg when his start on his mission had been so long delayed—that look which saw no hard or hindering circumstance, but only the distant and splendid goal.

His compassion was all for others when he looked upon Ethan's fields, where seed had rotted in the cold, wet ground, or had sprung up in thin, pale growth, only to be beaten upon by hail-storms or deluges of rain. Even if the weather improved there could now be only the scantiest of crops, and people and animals must suffer many privations.

When skies are unkind the husbandman must work all the harder for what may be saved, so Johnny was out, now, bringing a wonderful store of practical wisdom and skill to Ethan's help. He guided the plow, swung the scythe, repaired tools and harness, followed the sheep on the hills, led the men of the neighborhood to a grassy marsh where wild forage might be cut to eke out their scanty meadows, and brought in the winter's supply of fuel. So he won back, if not his old, tireless strength, at least his old, well-directed energy, and fitted himself to take up his inspired task again. But as he said nothing about this, Ethan and Mary thought that even his mission was fading from his memory. They had a feeling of happy security that he would remain with them in contentment. Capable as he was of doing his own work, he showed an increasing unfitness to take care of himself.

It was in this year of profound discouragement and ruinous losses, when men had to sacrifice stock they could not feed, and go into debt for high-priced seed brought up from the South, that Johnny lost something of the natural man's instinct of self-preservation. His spirit of brotherly love pushed him over the verge of reason into those eccentric and endearing forms of self-sacrifice which ever afterward marked him. Because it had been necessary for men to do so when animals were on short rations, he continued to carry heavy loads, and to walk long distances, to spare horses. He refused to eat, even at tables generously supplied, until sure that women and children had had enough, and he gave his clothing to any ill-clad stranger whom he met on the road.

And, seeing how hard plants and low animal orders struggled against extinction, his sympathy and reverence for all life developed into a poetic and fantastic consideration. An earthworm drowned out of its burrow, a bee made sluggish by cold rain, became a piteous thing. He pruned trees like a surgeon, only to heal some ill, insisting that they could feel the cruel knife; and he was sure that seeds were moved by thought and emotion, as they lay in pulsing germination in the dark.

Again there were but ten days of Indian summer, and winter set in so early and severe that, by the middle of December, wagons were driven across the frozen Ohio. But while the weather was intensely cold, there were few storms and little snow, and the ice went out in February with such destructive floods as had never before been recorded. All Western streams were choked with wreckage, and towns were cabled to trees on the bluffs. Then, as the water subsided, the bottoms were spread with rich alluvia, and the season leaped into genial spring. As if by magic the ground thawed and dried out for the plowing in March. The birds, sadly diminished in number but mad with joy, arrived early and raised an extra brood that golden summer, as if aware that they must restore nature's disturbed balance.

In Johnny's veins, too, the sap of spring ascended. He brought in the new-born lambs to the fire. He spaded the flower-beds and kitchen garden. From fruit-tree and shrub he cut away dead wood and parasitic suckers. As the sunny, showery days of April went by he had many secret sources of happiness about which those who loved him could only surmise. As though it were some unfolding drama, he watched the clustered buds of the apple-trees swell and swell until every little nosegay showed the pink edges of close-packed petals. He went to sleep one night on the bench in excited expectancy, and in the morning awoke to that miracle of spring —mounds and drifts and banks of rosy bloom, a blue ocean of incense, and the harmony of birds and bees.

Before he was awake Mary had slipped

out with Betty's little rocking-chair. For
long, speechless moments he gazed at it
swaying in the breeze, and at the blossoming
boughs shaking out their fluttering draperies
of pink and pearl. His breakfast was placed
before him on the rustic table, and gleeful
children tumbled out into the happy day.
And here was friendly, helpful, cheerful
Mary-go-'round sitting beside him with a bit
of sewing. He startled her by remarking
that the trees were so lovely because it was
their wedding-day, and told her something
of the fertilization of the blossoms by the
bees. But when the thought had dwelt in
her mind a moment, she said:

"That is beautiful!" She blushed like any
bride, and sat for a time in tender reverie.
"Ethan and I were married under the apple-
blossoms. Think of being canopied with
bliss in such an hour!"

By and by she asked, "Johnny, do you
remember how you used to take us children
on a journey 'round the world?"

Yes, he remembered, with a pleasure as
great as hers. There were little ones here
to-day—no break now, to him, in the flow
of the generations. The hours went by in the

old manner of Betty's time. He got a scythe and mowed the grass, and he fetched out the big table for the picnic dinner. Then, yielding to tugging hands and coaxing voices, he took the littlest baby on his back and marched away at the head of a procession, for such brave and laughing adventure as would make them say, when they grew up, "Don't you remember?" When Mary heard them scrambling on all-fours, and squealing like bear cubs under the shrubbery, she cried for pure happiness.

Johnny was having his old day in Paradise with Betty and her little brood.

They were not surprised in the morning to find that he was gone, but, more than a little anxious, Ethan followed him, unseen, for two days. Mary ran down the road to meet him on his return, and Ethan dropped from his horse to walk with her.

"It's all right, Mary. I watched Johnny go into farm-houses and villages all bowered in his orchards. The country never looked more beautiful. And such welcomes! Men and women, children and dogs, ran across fields and down the lanes to meet him. He will come back when the trees are done blooming, and there will be no harm in his taking such a holiday at any time. He has a friend in every person, a home under every roof in Ohio."

When the scented snow of faded petals was drifting on every wind, Johnny reappeared. He came in out of the dewy dusk, to stand erect in the doorway, his feet in bark sandals, his head minus a covering, his silver hair and beard a frame for a face of burning zeal and unquenchable youth, to announce a bit of news which had thrilled his heart and the heart of all America seven years before.

"The Erie Canal has been opened! Thousands of people are pouring over Lake Erie into the woods and prairies of Michigan and Indiana. Ohio does not need me now. I am going out there to plant orchards."

XIII

THE SHINING GOAL

H E talked for an hour, pouring forth such a torrent of eloquence that, when he took his blankets to the bench in the orchard, he left them thrilled and uplifted.

"It was as though he had been up on a mountain, talking with God." Mary's voice shook and her eyes were wet. "But we cannot let him go. He would die in some wretched, lonely way."

"I don't believe it; but what if he should?" Ethan had been carried off his firmly planted Yankee feet, as by the sound of trumpets and drums. It was the man's point of view: courage and faith were equipment for any task; and life was the thing—the vision, the adventure. The woman must hold fast to the good already gained.

"But, Ethan, Johnny is growing old!"

"He doesn't know it. He never will know it. Don't you dare tell him." The tone was exultant. It had been an unforgetable experience to see consecration rekindle the fires of youth.

"That's just it. He lives in a dream—"

"It's a brave dream that will make him work to the last day of his life as if inspired. I hope he'll never wake up. Mary, what has he lost, after all? Except for a measure of his physical strength, nothing that would ever be of any use to him. And, like most men of his wiry build and active mind, he has a wonderful vitality that will stand him in good stead. What a world this would be if we could all be delivered from self-distrust and fear—forget the things that paralyze effort; age and failure, sickness and sorrow."

"That's a beautiful thing to see in Johnny, but you know, Ethan, that he is incapable of taking care of himself. If anything dreadful happened to him it would break the heart of the West."

"No, it would not. The West would glory in him. Johnny has in him the stuff of heroes and martyrs, and such men are not to be

313

held back. He loved your dear, sweet mother, and the tragedy of it has finally turned his brain, but that had no power to hold him from the work to which he was called in his youth. And how are we to hold him? Have we the right? If we meddle in this he would die, after a few, miserable, wasted years. We could not bear that, Mary. I think we must have the courage to let him go."

She suddenly surrendered. "I know. I knew it all the time he was talking, but was not reconciled." Then her eyes, too, glowed as if with reflection from Johnny's soul of flame. "Did you ever see any one as jubilant? Such light is not to be hidden under a bushel. It is to be set on a hilltop for all the world to witness!"

Something of Johnny's own spirit sustained them in the months of waiting for the ripening of seed; and any lingering doubts of the wisdom and kindness of their resolve were dispelled as his energy and happiness mounted with the sun. An orchardist, he knew supremely how to wait, and wings were given to time by his moral necessity of filling every possible hour with useful work. But even if he had not been the busiest person on the

314

farm, he would not have been impatient to be off. Not since he left Pittsburg a generation before had he spent the dramatic season of growth in one orchard; and this dear plantation which he had twice set out for Betty's earthly paradise was haunted, now, by her gentle shade. Companioned by the beloved dead whom he confused with the living, every day of time was but a blissful moment of eternity.

Morning and evening and in the noon-hour of rest he watched the small, green hips form as the petals fell, and, through genial weeks and months, expand to their full roundness. As the equal nights came on with turbulent weather, he was often awakened by the vigorous threshing of the trees and the mellow dropping of the windfalls. The apples filled so with bursting juices that their skins were stretched to a satiny luster, as thin, fine-grained and defensive as gold-beater's parchment; and all the moods of summer and the alchemy of earth and sun were condensed in every little painted sphere, and the very breath of the Creator was hidden in the seed.

And then, cider-making time on the pioneer

farm! The cattle were out on the dwindling pastures. The corn stood in brown shocks in the fields, with frost-rimed pumpkins lying like harvest moons in the stubble. Multi-colored leaves sifted down through the drowsy air of Indian summer. The small press, a rude, home-made but competent affair, was set up in the orchard, where every tree, so irregularly planted, so individual of growth and habit, had a personality and an intimate history of its own.

The apples, not sorted as to kind, but only as to perfection and keeping quality, lay in variegated heaps of ruby and russet, green and gold, on the ground. The culls were pared, cored and cut up for the big kettle of cider-apple butter which was made out of doors, over the brick oven or a gipsy fire; or they were tumbled pell-mell into the hopper of the press. As the amber juice gushed out it was drunk at once from a gourd or tin dipper, boiled and sealed in bottles for use in mince pies, or was turned into the vinegar-barrel. The choicest fruit was stored in bins in cool, dark, cellars, or was buried in pits lined with bright straw. No child needed a light to find his favorite variety. He could burrow and fetch up the most elusive by the feel of it in his hand, and his nose would confirm his judgment. Now the north wind might blow, the robin fly south and Johnny be out on some bleak road, but there would be comfort and pleasure of his providing at the winter fireside.

The whole family helped him wash the seeds out of the pomace and dry them on the chimney-shelf. From the wagon-gate they watched and waved to him until, with the long stride which carried him so rapidly over great distances, he disappeared around a bend of the road. The hearts of Ethan and Mary went with Johnny along every mile of that brave journey, whose limit was the length of days allotted to him and the goal an orchard on the utmost horizon.

Their forethought went with him, too. Mary had spent time and reflection on a letter to Dr. Hildreth. It was the right of the people of the West, who loved him, to know how it was with Johnny. As capable as he had ever been of doing his beautiful work, his own safety and comfort must now be a charge on those he had served so long and so unselfishly. People were prepared for his changed appearance, his lapse of memory, his extravagant mysticism, and the exaggerated sympathies which impelled him to strip himself of the necessaries of life. They were asked not to recall to him the sad things which he had forgotten, to indulge his consoling beliefs, attend to his physical needs, and have the courage and faith to let him go on.

In Marietta the letter passed from hand to hand. Men talked about it in thoughtful groups on the street, and women parted with misty eyes at garden gates. Copies of it were made, and sent on to other towns. Copied again and again, Mary's letter went 'round from Pittsburg to the prairies, reminding every one who had an orchard, and every one for whom he lived only to replant the orchard that had been destroyed, of the debt of love and gratitude that was owed to Johnny. There was no waterway or post-road or wild trail in the region which did not ring with his name; no child who did not listen wide-eyed to his brave and tender story; no family shrine from which a prayer did not go up that his days might be long in the land and his pathway lined with his own blossoming trees. In thinking of him the social and religious conscience was awakened, and other men and women were stirred to neglected civic and neighborly duties. Thus, while still living, Johnny became a poignant and admonishing memory.

And if it had been a startling thing to the people of a generation before to see the gentle, zealous and undefended youth, it was now an arresting and uplifting experience to have this fervid and unconsciously aging man come in, erect under his beneficent burden, clad in any insufficient and nondescript way, his white hair streaming in the winter wind. It was as though the bitter frosts which had laid the blight of discouragement on so many had touched Johnny grievously, too, but only to strengthen his purpose and sweeten his spirit. A sermon and a song, he journeyed down the Scioto and Hocking valleys, and up the Muskingum. The grateful affection and respect in which he had always been held deepened to the reverent love which has been, everywhere and in every age of the world, accorded to moral superiority.

His was the honored place at board and fireside where, by many innocent deceptions, he was persuaded to accept the best. And, although few people had much surplus clothing, warm garments were always found for Johnny. He progressed rapidly and gleaned a great store of seeds, for now children helped him wash them out of the pomace; hero-worshiping farm and village boys tramped with him on every highway, assisting him over many a delaying difficulty, and when his leather bag grew heavy, men discovered that they had errands his way and gave him lifts in wagons. In not a few instances towns and churches took up collections and bought horses and new clothing for him. Such wealth, however, he held only in trust for the next needy stranger he encountered. So, in the course of a few years, people learned to supply his immediate necessities with anything of small value that was serviceable. And in Ohio, at least, where his errand kept him on main-traveled roads in the oldest and most thickly settled districts, he never suffered privation for a longer time than it took him to make the next house.

One day early in March he reappeared at the old home, "to spend the day with Betty." A neighboring farmer, returning from the

nearest village in a wagon, had picked him
up on the road, along which he was staggering under the weight of two big bags of seeds.
From a last year's scarecrow, fallen in a corn-
field, he had taken a crownless hat and a gun-
nysack coat. The winter of toil and travel
had stripped his spare figure of every ounce
of surplus flesh, and from his thin-featured,
ascetic face his large dark eyes shone, brilliant
and eager, from the urgency within.

"Johnny dear, you are half frozen!" Mary
cried. Quick tears filled her eyes. She never
could get used to seeing him come in like this.
She did not rest now until he was warmed
and fed, and clothed decently in one of Ethan's
good suits. He had trifling gifts for the children—marbles for the boys and bright hair-
ribbons for the little girls. It was in this way,
and for religious books to distribute among the
elders in scantily supplied cabins on the
prairies, that he spent the small sums of
money which many people slipped into his
pockets.

After supper, when the children were in
bed, Johnny and Mary and Ethan and the
little empty rocking-chair gathered around
the open fire in the old grouping. While

Mary knitted and Ethan shelled seed-corn Johnny read aloud from the New Testament and from the copy of Swedenborg which he always carried in the bosom of his shirt. At the end of every day, whether alone or in company, he had this sweet hour of communion and prayer. Wholly preoccupied, then, with the other world, he seemed to lose touch with earthly persons and things. To any audience, and with an astonishing poetic imagery drawn from his intimate knowledge and love of the most elusive things of nature, he described his visions and reported his talks with angels.

These fantastic accounts were listened to everywhere with pleasure, respect and even credulity. Johnny had a personal charm that was felt by every one, and a voice of beauty and persuasion, and when he spoke of his faith or his mission, which was faith transmitted into work, his speech was so inspired, his countenance so lighted with the fires of fanaticism, that people quite lost their sober judgment.

Mary and Ethan were carried away now when he sprang to his feet, swept his halo of silver hair back from his face, and, like any prophet of old, delivered his burning message. He was going into the wilderness, with no thought for the morrow, to take comfort and beauty to brave men, wistful women and defrauded children. Angels would watch over

SWEPT HIS HALO OF SILVER HAIR BACK FROM HIS FACE, AND, LIKE ANY PROPHET OF OLD, DELIVERED HIS BURNING MESSAGE

him, ravens feed him, manna fall from the skies. All the days of his life he would walk in safety, blessedness and peace until his task was done.

Their hearts sank. In the moment of re-action they looked at each other in sick dis-

may. Was this dear visionary, who was
"not all here" because a good part of him was
already in heaven, to be let go, perhaps to
wander about aimlessly in perilous wilds?
But almost at once they were reassured.
The part of him that was on earth was all
practical, informed, efficient. During the winter he had read the newspapers and talked
with leading men. He had overlooked no
detail by which he could give the greatest
service to the greatest number in his new
field, and with the least danger of his planting being brought to an untimely end.

Taking a bit of charred wood from the
hearth, he sketched a rough map of the old
Northwest Territory on Mary's white-pine
table. Then, with three swift strokes, he
marked the northwestward trend of migration, above the navigable streams of the Ohio
River Valley—the National Road which was
being pushed through the centrally located
capitals of the three Southern states to the
Mississippi; the post-road soon to be opened
between Detroit and Chicago; and the hundreds of miles of canals that were projected
along the Maumee, Miami and Wabash, to
connect Lake Erie with the Ohio River.

"Thousands of people are breaking those iron trails to the West and settling near them, and those are the routes I must follow. In another dozen years there will be tens of thousands. Then there will be towns and nurserymen. But in that time a generation of children could grow up without the memories of orchards."

A dozen years! He was fifty-eight, and in the hard, half-century of pioneering in the Middle West many were old at forty-five.

When he had gone to his comfortable bed in the loft chamber, Ethan could not contain his pride in him. "He'll do it, Mary. Johnny knows what he is about. He'll live long and finish that task. You might as well try to stop the Holy Ghost."

Mary had knelt and repeated the prayer she had learned at her mother's knee before she answered. "Whether his life be long or short, he will live the Beatitudes and see God every hour."

When Johnny rose at an early hour in the morning, Ethan brought a horse to the door for him—a big, strong animal that could carry him and his belongings with ease. He disposed his seeds, and the new tools and small camping outfit provided for him, on the horse, and spared a moment to give him the pleasure of nosing in a pocket for an apple. But when Ethan urged him to mount he shook his head. That was a heavy enough load for any horse. Not until there were orchards in his new field of labors would he look upon blossoming or fruiting trees again; nor could he stop every spring for a day with Betty. He often saw her, now, in some familiar or angelic guise, but it was only here that he fully recovered her.

"Is Betty asleep?"

"Yes, Johnny, she's asleep," Mary managed to answer, with a tender smile.

"Don't waken her."

He led the horse up to the road. They knew he would walk all that weary way, and that he was not likely to have this good horse for his baggage for any length of time. He would gradually strip himself of every comfort and advantage. So he would go to the end of his earthly journey, keeping only the essential things—his seeds, his tools, his love for Betty and his purpose.

At Sandusky he left the horse behind for an emigrant family stranded by the loss of an animal on the road, and crossed the cold lake to Detroit on the windy deck of a freight-boat. He had no recollection of having been there since the war of twenty years before, when the place was a lethargic, wilderness fortress and Indian trading-post. These hurrying crowds enchanted him—so many people for him to serve! Dragging his roped baggage across the gang-plank, he mounted the steps which led up from the dock.

Without help it would be difficult to go on. But help came to Johnny, now, when it was needed, and his relations with men were on the simple religious basis of the duty and joy of giving and receiving. With entire confidence he stood still and looked out over bobbing hats, piles of goods and a confusion of tangled trucks and teams, until he caught the serene and kindly eye of a French Récollet friar. The Franciscan missionary was evidently just starting on a journey, for he rode one pony and led another. Making his way through the press, he dismounted. It was a friend, whose face and name and habit of life were erased from his memory, who laid a fraternal hand on Johnny's shoulder.

"We go the same way, *mon frère*, and

upon much the same errand. So put your belongings on my extra animal and we will walk in company." Thinking it well that, in the midst of their temporal concerns, men should be reminded of their blessings, he raised his hand and voice. "Let us give thanks to Our Lady that Johnny Appleseed moon has risen on the woods and prairies."

A cheer went up from those within hearing and hats were thrown in the air. Johnny did not know that the hope of orchards had been cruelly dashed from the lips of the people of this region once, nor that the promise of his return had been glad tidings to settlers and an inducement to new-comers. The extravagant welcomes and consideration which greeted him seemed only the natural response to his own love and elation. Now his way to join the procession which was moving across the marshy ground to the West, was lined with cheers, hand-clasps, uncovered heads, lifted babies and faces which, at the sight of his white hair and eyes of consecrated and ardent youth, paid the silent tributes of hearts made suddenly humble. A hush fell upon the crowd for a moment as that passionate pilgrim disappeared in the forest.

THE SHINING GOAL

There were more people in the country than he had expected to find, and more corn and cattle. In many districts game practically disappeared after the winter of the deep snow, and in the hard years which followed farming was pursued with desperate energy. But, except on the road westward from Detroit, where the horn of the stage-coach to Chicago presently woke the echoes of the woods, it was another decade before traveling became safer or easier. Until the National Road and canals were opened, little could be brought into the country or sent out; and until near the middle of the century people who had settled at any distance from navigable water continued to live in the most primitive way.

In later years, and by chroniclers who suffered none of the hardships of the first generation in that region, much was made of Johnny's bare or bark-sandaled feet and his scant and nondescript garments. But very few people wore shoes in the summer months, and most were reduced to odd makeshifts in the way of clothing. What they had they shared with Johnny. And while he always gave away the best that was given to him, his condition was not piteous and all his eccentricities were endearing. The hemp-bag shirt and pasteboard hat in which he appeared at times, were robe and crown for a new St. John of the wilderness.

As far as was possible he was watched and guarded, for in the care of himself Johnny was "plumb foolish." Sublimely delivered from fear, he waded bare-legged across any snake-infested swamp which lay in his path; and, filled with reverence and compassion for all life, he refused to build a camp-fire where ants had their underground villages or moths were flying. He had been known to feed a sick wolf which followed him like a dog, and to put out a fire he had made against a hollow log in which he discovered a hibernating bear, and to sleep near by in the dark.

But no harm ever befell him, a thing to be accounted for only by his own belief that he was under Divine protection. His endurance, too, was nothing less than a miracle. Year after year, while he withered and wrinkled like any winter apple losing its juices by slow evaporation, but sound and sweet to the last, he covered hundreds of miles of country, and was never known to be ill. When the earth stiffened with frost he went out to his gleaning of seeds through Toledo, and he returned to his planting through Detroit, Fort Wayne or the Quaker settlements of eastern Indiana before ever a prairie furrow was turned up to the sun. In his annual rounds one of his sources of happiness was to note how the children, colts and calves, and his own little trees, playing in wind and sun, grew tall and strong to take up the sober duties and higher joys of life.

Before the first of Johnny's trees in that region were in bearing, beard had started through the tanned cheek of "Billy" grown to young William Worth. When he had fenced in a quarter-section of prairie on the riverbank north of Fort Wayne, broken the sod for corn and built a little white cot, he asked Johnny to plant an orchard for Madeleine Bourie. The house was of the style that was dear to the French trader from the province of Quebec. Long and low, its roof, which sloped out over a narrow front veranda, was set with tiny dormer windows. When its clapboards were whitewashed, honeysuckles and Prairie Queen roses trained up the porch posts, and Lombardy poplars planted to flank the picket-gate, it was a pleasant home indeed to come upon at the end of a day's journey. Johnny always slept there one night when he passed through the town. And for Madeleine, who had the brown hair, blue eyes and engaging manners of her Norman race, he laid out a garden and orchard patterned after the old home of his heart in Ohio.

Suddenly, in a thousand scattered places, Johnny's earliest trees bloomed and fruited. The wilderness fell back, abashed. Birds and bees came in from the woods. Cabins which had been but rude and unloved shelters in bitter lands of exile, were transformed into homes overnight, and people took root in wild soil tamed by these domestic trees. His orchards bore other crops besides apples — beauty, contentment, the hope of better days, the social gathering, memories. Year after year his trees increased in number and in value, for grafting-buds were taken from old orchards in Detroit, Piqua and Dayton, and gradually carried westward. When the new trade routes were opened Johnny had nurseries in market-towns to turn over to other men. The dozen years were more than gone, and he had finished this task. But there were other fields for his planting—farther horizons.

He was seventy-two years old when, in the spring of 1847, his eager feet took the path of blossoms up the Valley of the Maumee toward the new goal. Early in March he stopped at the old home for his day with Betty, so buoyant, so full of happy plans for his new undertaking in the northwestern corner of Indiana, that, although he was looking very old and feeble, Mary and Ethan gave up their intention of trying to persuade him to remain with them and end his days in comfort. His comfort, his spiritual necessity, was in his continuing task. For him time was merged in eternity. When his work on earth was done there would be orchards for his planting and nurturing in the Garden of God. In going up through the Black Swamp, in a soft and foggy thaw, he had a mild attack of malaria. He managed to reach Toledo, but only to lie in bed there for a month. Bewildered by the prostration which had so slight a cause, and by the trembling weakness and shortness of breath that paralyzed effort when he was up again, he crept out into the warm sunshine of a late April day, to look upon trees that were on the point of bursting into bloom.

The planting season would be over before he could reach his new field, and friends pleaded with him to remain where he was for the summer to recover his strength. He did consent to send his seeds and tools to Fort Wayne by canal-boat, but, for himself, he meant to walk. A leisurely tramp up that happy valley in apple-blossom-time would be a holiday, and it would set him on his feet again for his summer of exploration.

What a transformation had been wrought in this valley by the courage and faith and killing labor of two generations of men! It thrilled Johnny's heart to think of the share he had had in that brave work. Even a decade before this hundred-mile depression had been all but impassable in the spring; and a flatboat voyage down the dark-walled, sluggish flood in the autumn, when he had put in his seeds, had been a dismal experience. Now, Toledo had pulled itself up out of the mud, and, a garden-girt city of four thousand people, stood on its green peninsula, between the shipping on the bay and the barges on the canal, taking its rich toll of travel and trade. There were still stretches of swampy woods that came right down to the towpath, but for the most part the low plain lay open to the view. From high banks along the rapids a wayfarer could look down upon miles of foaming waters, and running back from every busy little bowered town, the prairies stretched from swell to swell, between belts of woodland, with corn-fields, meadows and comfortable homes hidden in bloom.

Going up that valley was like a vision of the road to heaven and what lay at the end of it, which had once enchanted him. Along the bank of a full-flowing river he had followed a path of blossoms, until he had come to gleaming gates of morning opening on limitless fields of spring, with mounds and banks of bloom on every horizon. And in a secluded paradise of ordered loveliness he had found Betty, restored to her youthful beauty, and weaving garlands for the shining heads of the little children gathered around her.

Every hour he was obliged to rest. Kind people, he noticed, were very apt to join him and to keep him company for a stage of the journey. If alone, he gathered the harvest of the poetic eye and ear. He ate in any doorway, slept wherever he happened to be at nightfall—for every roof was a home for him; but he was off again before any one else was stirring. Little ones sent to call him to breakfast ran back, disappointed.

"Oh, mother, Johnny's gone!"

The older people looked at each other across cheerful tables sadly. Many who watched Johnny moving slowly up the valley, as if in a happy dream, did not expect ever to see him again; and they waited anxiously to hear that he had reached Fort Wayne.

It was near sunset one evening, when the blossoms were white with age, that Madeleine Worth, busy in her kitchen, heard the picket-gate click on the latch. She ran down the path to meet Johnny. Although weary and faint that he tottered to a fall, his eyes still had that undying look of his far-away youth, as of one who sees only the distant and splendid goal.

"Did my seeds come?"

"A week ago. You should have come with them. We have been afraid— Dear friend, you have been ill!"

"It was nothing—not worth mentioning. I will be better soon."

Under cover of clasping her firm young hands about his arm as fondly as any grand-

HIS EYES STILL HAD THAT UNDYING LOOK OF HIS FAR-AWAY YOUTH, AS OF ONE WHO SEES ONLY THE DISTANT AND SPLENDID GOAL

daughter, Madeleine helped him up the steps. He sank breathlessly into the armed chair of hickory splints. In a moment she brought

337

out a bowl of hot milk, and said that he should have fresh eggs and wheat-bread toast and apple-blossom honey for his supper, because he was "company." Tucking bright calico cushions around him, she left him and, with misty eyes, returned to her work of preparing the evening meal.

He sat there blissfully, watching the loosened petals blow before the wind, and listening to the vesper songs of the birds and the laughing chatter of the very young children who had a bark playhouse in the orchard. He was never alone now. Old friends returned, thronging the sacred room of memory, as he looked out between the sentinel poplars, across the green and flowery prairie to the setting sun. He was asleep when William came in from the fields.

The boy who had said, "You lean on me, Johnny; I'm strong," was now a man to lean upon. A stalwart pioneer of the second generation, in his youthful prime, he looked down upon Johnny, sunk among the cushions —wasted to emaciation, bleached to transparency, worn out by his half-century-long labor of love! William could not eat his supper for the lump in his throat. He made up his mind that Johnny's wanderings should come to an end. He would be unable to travel at all for some days, and he and his clever Madeleine must find a way to keep him altogether.

Rested and refreshed, Johnny's soul of flame burned with its old heat and brightness for an hour. People were going into northwestern Indiana, settling on the sand-dunes and in the oak-openings of the old lands of the Pottawatomies; around the shores of the many lovely lakes that dotted the northern prairies, and on the rich plains which bordered the southern margin of that million-acre mystery, the swamps of the Kankakee. Most of them would be sixty miles from any outlet. He might go on to the vast prairies of eastern Illinois. In another dozen years—

He wanted to take a blanket to the orchard, but clouds had spread across the sky and the soft wind felt like rain, so he was persuaded to sleep on a pallet on the porch floor. Once in the night William came out with an extra covering, and found him asleep.

Before daylight he awoke suddenly. In his dream he had heard the old boat-bugle of early days on the Ohio River—distant, ineffable, such as had seemed to call the soul of Mary Lake to life everlasting. It was not yet morning, but the rain had ceased. He could have an hour in the orchard before starting on the journey to his new field of labor. When his heart had quieted down from its wild beating he took up his seeds and tools and went down the steps into the odorous darkness.

He may have slept, to dream again, for he thought himself in another, dearer orchard. Some happy memory made him smile when the breeze shook down a shower of drops and of cool, scented petals on his upturned face. At the back of the house the meadow sloped to the grassy bank of the river. He could see the stream which still lay dark, and the rosy drift of dawn which bloomed above it.

The first rays of morning light were reflected from the fluttering leaves of the wet poplars. The prairie was spread out, gray, then silver, with beaded rain. There was a twittering in the tree-tops. A meadow-lark fluted from the pasture. Madeleine, coming out to call Johnny to breakfast, saw his empty bed, with startled blue eyes that filled with tears.

THE SHINING GOAL

"Oh, Billy, he's gone!"

But no trail was broken across the drenched grass of the prairie, where the rising sun awoke a sea of sparkles.

Johnny was gone, to an eternal day with Betty, and to plant orchards in the Garden of God.

www.ingramcontent.com/pod-product-compliance
Lightning Source LLC
Chambersburg PA
CBHW010858090426
42738CB00018B/3433